I'll Always Have Paris

A Memoir

***Also by Art Buchwald
in Large Print:***

Leaving Home
Lighten Up, George
Whose Rose Garden Is It Anyway!
I Think I Don't Remember
"*You* Can *Fool All of the People All of the
    Time*"
While Reagan Slept

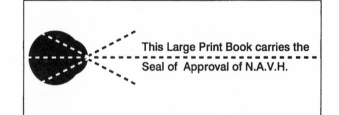

This Large Print Book carries the
Seal of Approval of N.A.V.H.

I'll Always Have Paris

A Memoir

Art Buchwald

Thorndike Press • Thorndike, Maine

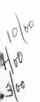

"Be the Best of Whatever You Are" by Douglas Malloch, copyright 1926 by Scott Dowd, copyright renewed 1954 by Helen M. Malloch.

Published in 1996 by arrangement with G.P. Putnam's Sons.

Thorndike Large Print ® Basic Series.

The tree indicium is a trademark of Thorndike Press.

The text of this Large Print edition is unabridged.
Other aspects of the book may vary from the original edition.

Set in 16 pt. Bookman Old Style.

Printed in the United States on permanent paper.

Library of Congress Cataloging in Publication Data

Buchwald, Art.
    I'll always have Paris : a memoir / Art Buchwald.
      p. cm.
    ISBN 0-7862-0842-2 (lg. print : hc)
    ISBN 0-7862-0843-0 (lg. print : sc)
    1. Buchwald, Art — Homes and haunts — France — Paris.
2. Paris (France) — Social life and customs — 20th century.
3. Humorists, American — 20th century — Biography.
4. Journalists — France — Paris — Biography. 5. Americans
— France — Paris — Biography. I. Title.
[PS3503.U1828469 1996b]
814'.54—dc20
[B]   96-9844

Dedication

Just before she died in July 1994, I told my wife, Ann, that I was dedicating this book to her. She asked me why, and I said, because Paris belonged to both of us. The book was our story — not just mine.

She accused me of trying to make her feel better. I denied it and said, "I can't write about my life without including you as the star."

She sighed. "If it will make you happy, go ahead."

Writing this book took longer than I expected, and Ann didn't live to see it completed, although I read passages to her on my daily visits to show her how it was coming along.

Paris had been the scene of our happiest moments and, after a short while, I found that she looked forward to correcting my facts and adding details that I had forgotten.

Those last days were very precious. Paris brought us together in the beginning and it brought us together at the end.

Contents

Merci Beaucoup

Not all computers are friendly. The one that I used to write this book seemed to be the unfriendliest of all. Paragraphs were transposed and pages of subject matter disappeared into thin air. The person responsible for bringing any sense of order out of all this was my assistant, Jeannie Aiyer. She devoted her days, evenings, and weekends to questioning, clarifying, and editing everything I wrote. Her advice was invaluable and I thank her very much.

Two other people to whom I say "merci beaucoup" are Neil Nyren and Phyllis Grann, my editors at Putnam's. I have leaned on them heavily.

Ursula Naccache, my secretary from the Paris years, was also particularly helpful. Ursula knew all my secrets and was in a unique position to comment on the material.

Author's Note

The city of Paris was founded in 52 B.C. Nothing much happened there until June 12, 1948, when I crashed Hemingway's moveable feast.

This is the second part of my memoirs and covers the years that I lived in Paris. The first book told about my youth and I called it Leaving Home.

Until this moment, my life had been a series of zigs and zags. Soon after I was born, my mother was confined to a mental institution, where she remained for thirty-five years. With my three sisters, I was placed in the Hebrew Orphan Asylum in New York, and then boarded out with foster parents.

At an early age, I discovered that I could make kids laugh, and in exchange they would think that I was a nice person. This worked pretty well until I ran away to join the U.S. Marine Corps in 1942. The Corps is not impressed with anyone who can make people laugh.

After serving in the Pacific for three years, I signed up with the G.I. Bill at the University of Southern California, which I attended for three years, before discovering that I could study in Paris, courtesy of the U.S. government. To my mind there was no choice. I quit life as a Trojan and set my sights on France. . . .

Chapter 1

I Arrive

In that spring of 1948, I hitchhiked to New York from California, and bought a one-way ticket on the *Marine Jumper*, a rusty, battered World War II troopship. At the dockside I bid farewell to my father and sisters, promising them that when I returned from France, I would be the most important writer in our country, or its equivalent.

The departure was typical of our family good-byes.

My sister Edith was certain that the ship was really heading for Israel and that I was going to fight in the first war for independence. My father presented me with a large bag of food from the Gaiety Delicatessen, which included corned beef, salami, brisket, cheeses, pickles, coleslaw, potato salad, chocolate cookies, and cream soda.

It was the perfect parental gesture, because my father and I had always found it easiest to show our feelings for one another with food. Three days out to sea, as we tried to subsist on the ship's cuisine, all my shipmates blessed him time and time again for his bon voyage gift.

The family was full of good advice. Alice, my oldest sister, warned me not to drink the water. Doris, who'd served as a nurse in the army, told me not to make love to French girls unless I was wearing protection.

Edith told me, "Carry your passport at all times and don't tell strangers that you're an American, because the French hate them."

A half hour later, as hundreds of parents stood on the dock waving, the *Marine Jumper*'s horn blew a mournful farewell, which, once we were at sea, I realized indicated that she was in pain.

The ship was loaded with fresh-faced American students — budding Pulitzer Prize winners, eager painters, future geniuses of the arts and sciences, as well as children of extremely successful businessmen.

We were the stepchildren of Gertrude

Stein, F. Scott Fitzgerald, Henry Miller, and Ezra Pound. We carried hardly any luggage, but if we'd ever declared our dreams to French customs, they would have been worth thousands of dollars in duty.

Since it was impossible to stay below, we spent most of the trip on deck lounging around. Unlike the troopship that had taken me to the Pacific, there was no one to tell us what to do, because we were paying passengers and were not to be pushed around.

Ships are great places to take stock of one's accomplishments. Gazing over the rail, it's easy to reflect on the past and ponder the future.

I was overwhelmed by a feeling that I was going to a place that was more intoxicating than anything I had ever dreamed of in the Marines or at USC. I had no fear then of what was to come, or even of failing at it, because I had no idea what I would be failing at. In the back of my mind, I thought I would become a writer — mainly because writing came easily to me and I didn't need a college degree to pursue it — but that was about it.

Aside from that, there was no time

limit on my stay in Europe. I could remain in Paris for a year on the G.I. Bill, and at the end of that time, I assumed, I could get a job if I wanted to stay. There was no love interest in my life, so I had no obligations to anyone. I felt good about that.

Several people had briefed me on Paris. A G.I. buddy who had spent several weeks there on leave from one of General Patton's tank outfits had spoken with authority. "The French are crazy over nylons, cosmetics, and chocolates. Most of the toilets in France have no seats and you have to stand up to do everything. Paris is full of pickpockets and money changers who will steal you blind. Most important, you always have to tip the usher who seats you in a movie house, or she'll break your knees with a flashlight."

It seemed like solid information, although some of it was not necessarily pertinent to my plans.

As we approached Le Havre, the port city displayed all the scars of war. The harbor was filled with sunken vessels and the area was alive with the sound of repair work and ships' horns. As the *Marine Jumper* slowly made its way to the pier, the student next to me raised a Coca-Cola in a toast and said, "We are here to thank Lafayette for giving us French toast."

"And French-fried potatoes," said Dick Gelb, a Yalie sporting a sweater with a very large *Y* on it.

"And French leave," his brother Bruce said.

Robert Ginna added, "Let's not forget French kissing."

We were ready to disembark — young men who would soon grow Ernest Hemingway beards, young women who would eagerly wear tight denim pants. We were about to claim our chairs in sidewalk cafés in one of the loveliest and most civilized cities in the world. We would never be the same again. The memories of the years, months, or even weeks we spent here would remain with us all our lives. Even those who could not speak the language would absorb the culture and learn a way of life that was unlike anything we had ever experienced.

It could have been the best of times or the worst of times, but one thing was certain — it was the only time we had.

This seems to be the right place to

mention a nagging skeleton in my closet. When I made the decision to study in France, I spoke no French. I assumed that I would be there only for a short time, and so there was no reason to learn it, since I possessed a U.S. passport and American travelers' checks. As the years went by, I never did learn the language but depended instead on an improvised Franglais which consisted of French and English and a great deal of body language, hand-waving, and shoulder-shrugging. It worked well, and I managed to survive without any serious problems. In fact, whenever I spoke their language, the French took pity on me and helped me out.

As I walked out of the Gare St-Lazare at about nine o'clock in the evening that day, my first impression of Paris was that it wasn't so much a city as a stage setting from a Broadway musical. The sidewalk cafés were exactly as they were depicted in the magazines and movies. There were honking taxis, street vendors selling dirty pictures, roses, oriental rugs, black-market money-changers from Corsica, men peddling carved-ivory ornaments from who-knows-where, begging gypsies with babies on their shoulders, and, finally, heavily rouged streetwalkers willing to sell sexual gratification for a price.

I slept in a hotel which, the next morning, I discovered, rented most of its rooms by the hour, except for a few tourists like me. It was very quaint, and my fondest memory of it was of hearing a noise in the hall at three A.M. and seeing a naked Chinese man screaming because someone wouldn't let him back into his room.

The following day, I headed for the Place de l'Opéra, where the American Express office and Café de la Paix were located, and where all the tourists hung out. I savored every moment of it. I knew no one, but I didn't feel alone.

That first week, I began writing letters at the sidewalk cafés to the people back home, not only describing the scene but telling many lies about how I was doing.

This one was saved by my friend Bob Markay:

"Dear Bob,

"I am in Paris and I got a great buy on a French beret. The sidewalk salesman told me that it had belonged to his

17

grandfather, who posed for Van Gogh's most famous self-portrait.

"My money is still holding out. The secret is French bread and French cheese. It is a banquet and all I need to keep me going.

"I haven't fallen in love yet, as I've decided to play hard to get. If a French baroness drives by and asks me to jump into her car, I will tell her, 'I prefer to walk.' And then add, 'Just because I am an American student, I have no intention of going to Maxim's and drinking a bottle of champagne with you and letting you take advantage of me in the back of your limousine.'

"I am constantly in touch with the arts. I have been to the Louvre and the Rodin museums, and Napoleon's Tomb. Because of my French beret, no one knows I am an American. As a matter of fact, I have been stopped by tourists who were lost and wanted to find their way. I deal with this in the same way as the French — I refuse to answer them.

"Am I homesick? Not really. It's amazing how fast you can forget the USC-Notre Dame game when you're in Paris."

A letter written to my sisters was far

more decorous. They lived in constant fear that I would return to the U.S. with a French wife and six babies.

Since I was using up what little money I had, my next step was to move out of the hotel and find a place to live. A boyhood friend named Buddy Plate, from Public School 35 in Hollis, Queens, lived in Montmartre, and I looked him up. He had become a wild abstract artist and was living with a Communist girlfriend in a tiny apartment. The place consisted of a bedroom, a dining room, a kitchenette, and a toilet with no bath. It was in Place Clichy, in a working-class neighborhood of Paris, far from the glamorous Right and Left Bank neighborhoods where Americans hung out. It would only cost me five dollars a month, however, and Buddy said I could have it for the summer, as he and his girlfriend were going away. I considered the offer more than generous. It was extremely romantic, and a perfect starting place for a young writer to begin the great American novel.

Buddy had been one of my closest friends and the first celebrity I had ever known. He was one of triplets, along with a sister named Betty and a brother named Billy. There were no other triplets at P.S. 35 or in the neighborhood, so VIP visitors to the school insisted on seeing them. The guests would walk into the classroom, and Buddy, Betty, and Billy would be asked to stand up. When I met Buddy again in Paris, he told me that he had always wanted to throw ink on them.

Although the triplets lived with an aunt, they also had a father who was a bookie. This made them even more exciting. The only time I met their father, he showed me a fistful of dollars. It was the most money I had ever seen.

Buddy had been an artist even in his grammar-school days. We had both been members of the "gang" — seven of us who did everything together. We'd smoked cigarettes, tried to cop feels from girls, listened to Glenn Miller records, and played all the sports. The best and brightest of us had been Harvey Carlson, who was killed in the Battle of the Bulge.

During those carefree days in Hollis, I never dreamed that Buddy would solve my housing problems in Paris when I grew up.

* * *

For someone who knew no French and who came from the hated United States, I was treated very well by everyone in Clichy.

I shopped in the food stalls carrying a string bag and pointing out what I wished to buy with a grin on my face. I said "Bonjour" to everyone on the street and I offered cigarettes to the neighbors when they stopped to talk to me.

My street could have been a painting by Utrillo. The outside of the apartment buildings had not been painted in years. It was summer, so all the windows were open, and women hung out of them talking to their neighbors or screaming at their children. In the early morning and late at night, they screamed at their husbands.

I fantasized that someday tourist buses would drive down my tiny street, and the tour guide with the microphone would announce, "This is the building where the Nobel Prize writer Art Buchwald wrote his best-selling autobiography, which he dedicated to his last lover, the singer Edith Piaf. When something didn't work for

21

him, he tore the paper out of his type-writer, crushed it up, and threw it into the cemetery over there. When Buchwald died, he asked that all the papers he threw away be cremated and the ashes scattered over the Académie Française."

As soon as I settled in, I applied for the G.I. Bill at the Veterans Administration located in the U.S. Embassy on the Place de la Concorde. I chose to study at the Alliance Française, one of the most popular French language schools in Paris for foreigners. It was located in a large brownstone house on the boulevard Raspail near boulevard Montparnasse, and they guaranteed that you could learn the language in three months.

An unfortunate incident prevented me from ever learning French with any skill, however. I met an ex-G.I. on my first day of class. During a smoking break, he said to me, "The gal who takes attendance every morning can be bribed."

"How so?"

"For a thousand francs [two dollars] a month, she will mark you present."

"You mean you don't have to go to

school, and you can still be on the G.I. Bill?"

"That's correct. If all the G.I.s in Paris who are supposed to be enrolled went to class, they would need a soccer stadium to accommodate them."

The G.I. pointed out the woman to me, and I said to her, "I'll bet you a thousand francs that you won't know when I'm in school, and when I am not."

She didn't even smile. She just took my thousand francs and walked away. Relieved of going to French language school (something I have always regretted, by the way), I continued my existence as a tourist. Through the grapevine, I heard that as an American I was entitled to gasoline stamps in exchange for dollars. I didn't have to own a car to get them. Gas coupons were as good as money in 1948, and I managed to sell mine to taxi drivers for $25 or $30 a month. So with $75 from the G.I. Bill, and $25 from gasoline stamps, I was as rich as a French fiddler on the roof.

Despite this new-found sensation of apparent wealth, when it came to spending money on dates, I was as frugal as I could be. If a woman wanted to go Dutch, I silently rejoiced. American daughters who received large infusions of money from their parents did not get insulted when we split the bill. At USC, if I had even hinted that a coed pay for her coffee, she would have pushed me out of her speeding convertible.

The sidewalk café was still one of the best places for me to meet people. It was not only a fresh air experience, but I always found someone willing to listen to my story. I never varied the telling of it. I told how I had turned my back on millions of dollars in Hollywood to become a struggling writer in Paris. Even the hookers who sat at café tables were taken with my tale.

By accident I discovered that the best place to connect with dates was the Louvre Museum. Women of all nationalities went there alone because they considered it safe and assumed that anyone looking at the Tintoretto could be trusted.

Whenever I spotted someone who struck my fancy, I walked along with her through several salons without being fresh or forward. Finally, after she had become used to my presence, I would say, "No one could hold a candle to Rembrandt. It's too bad he couldn't pass his kidney stone and died in so much pain." Or, "I once read that Gauguin threw paint remover on his mistress in Tahiti for falling asleep on his best self-portrait, and she hit him in the head with his last bottle of cognac."

These were good icebreakers. If she liked Titian, I confessed that I had always worshipped him. If her heart beat faster when she gazed at a Velázquez, I would proclaim, "My mother sold the three we had in our kitchen." If she laughed, we would soon be sitting at a café, where we'd tell each other lies about ourselves. I'd assure my new friend that I was a serious person who could afford to live anywhere but chose instead to work in a garret in a Communist quarter of Paris and write about the workers rather than the rich Paris merchants, who gouged the tourists on the Rue de la Paix.

Then I would say, "I have never asked anyone this before, but would you like to see the attic inspired by *La Bohème?* It's located in Montmartre, and no woman has ever visited it. If you go, you must swear that it will be your secret, and when I become famous you will never reveal its location to anyone."

Most women responded that they would rather see Napoleon's Tomb — but once in a while one admitted to being curious, and I know it's conceited, but I like to think that it was the highlight of her trip to Europe. I never felt guilty about deluding my guests. My apartment was a most romantic spot for the tourists, and certainly one they couldn't get on any American Express tour. If my Louvre date didn't want to see my garret, it was fine with me. Instead, we walked along the Seine, taking pictures and buying posters, and we always departed friends.

Over the years, the Louvre and I became familiar companions. Whenever someone came to Paris, it was a regular stop. One Sunday, I went to the museum with a young struggling American writer named Peter Stone, who also lived in Paris. While we were walking around, Peter said, "I wonder what the record is for going through the Louvre."

"You mean taking in everything?"

"No, just looking at the three things

that everybody comes to see — the Winged Victory, the Mona Lisa and the Venus de Milo. It's no secret that many tourists whiz through glancing at the three works of art, and then go out shopping again. What do you think the record for doing that is?"

I pretended to look in a guidebook, and said, "It says here that the track record for the Louvre is six minutes and twelve seconds. It is held by a man known as the Swedish Cannonball, who, paced by his Welsh wife, did it on November 23, 1937."

"Let's try to beat it," Peter said.

"No one can break a six-minute Louvre," I declared.

"That's what people said about the four-minute mile," Peter replied.

We had nothing to lose, so the following Sunday Peter showed up, and I made a show of firing off a starting pistol. He dashed in around the Venus de Milo, then up the stairs past the Winged Victory, down to the Mona Lisa — and you always have to say something when you look at the Mona Lisa, and Peter said, "I know the guy who has the original." Peter then dashed out into a waiting taxi. I timed him at five minutes and fifty-six seconds. That record still stands.

Years later, the Louvre hired I. M. Pei to build an entrance in the form of a glass pyramid, which makes it impossible for a tourist to enter in less than three hours, thus preventing anyone from breaking the old record.

In spite of bragging to everyone back home about my Paris life, I wasn't making much progress on my book. I kept telling myself that I had to live in Paris for a long time before I wrote about it. I was thinking about a plot concerning a young man who comes to France but is flat-busted. His agent writes and tells him he has a job for him in Hollywood, writing for a Lassie picture. He tells his lady love that MGM is offering big bucks, but it also means that the writer is finished and has to admit that he failed. That's as far as I got. It was two pages, and when I think about it now, it was the perfect film for Eddie Murphy.

After I left Clichy at the end of the summer, I didn't see too much of Buddy, but we did have a chance meeting six months later at the Veterans Administration in the American Embassy.

I had started writing for the *Herald Tribune* (which I'll get to in a moment) and my byline was appearing with the column. The VA director remembered that I was registered as a student. He checked, and found out that I wasn't attending school, so he called me in to court-martial me.

Somehow he discovered that Buddy wasn't attending school, either, so he demanded to see him as well. By coincidence, we were both sitting on the same bench charged with the same crime.

I was ushered in first and accused of defrauding the government out of $75 a month. The director looked like the warden of a maximum security prison. He had a silver crew cut, cold, piercing eyes, and a pen that he kept snapping on the desk to beat time with the lecture he was giving me.

I stood before him with my head bowed, waiting to hear what sentence he would pronounce.

"You have committed a despicable act," he growled. "You have made a mockery of the Veterans Administration, you have made a laughing stock of the American taxpayer, and you have embezzled money from the United States Treasury."

"I'm sorry," I said. "What happens now?"

He explained that he could either send me to Leavenworth or recommend that I be given a veteran's dishonorable discharge. I asked what that meant. He slammed his hand on his desk. "You will never get a VA mortgage for the rest of your life!"

I pretended it was more punishment than I could possibly stand and backed out of his office, bowing in Japanese fashion.

"He's tough," I told Buddy. "He's a bloody bureaucrat. I'll wait for you."

Before I tell you what transpired next in the VA office, I have to clue you in on Buddy Plate's art. He stood five feet from the canvas and threw cans of paint all over it. He was openly contemptuous of people who claimed they understood his work. Buddy was a genius, but he painted to a different drummer.

When he went in, the director asked him to sit down, and offered him a cigar. Then they got down to business. The director said that he was sorry Buddy hadn't been attending classes.

At the same time, he understood that artists do not like to be told how to paint. The director said that he could forget the incident in exchange for a small favor. He had two daughters, named Heidi and Clara, and if Buddy would paint their portraits as a gift for their mother, the director would forget the whole thing.

Buddy asked what would happen if he refused. The director said, "I'll boot your ass out of Paris in five minutes."

Buddy came out of the office shaken. "He wants me to paint his kids' portraits."

"No sweat," I said. "Da Vinci did it for his VA director."

Buddy sat on the bench and held his head in his hands, and said, "I've sold out. I sold my soul for seventy-five dollars a month."

"It won't be too bad. Throw three cans of paint on the canvas and tell him that's his daughters."

"I can't do that. He says if he doesn't like the pictures, the deal is off."

I said, "At least you have a chance to keep your money — he cut me off at the knees. My sole support now comes from the *Herald Tribune* and that's twenty-five a week."

Buddy said, "Kipling was right. No one cares about the bloody soldier once the war is over."

I agreed. "All we are in Paris is cannon fodder."

Chapter 2

Hôtel des États-Unis

When the summer ended, I said farewell to my friends in the Clichy neighborhood. It was a sad moment for all of us. To them I was "le vrai Americain." Except for Buddy, I was the first one that they had ever met personally. They liked me because I told them that I didn't want to start a nuclear war, or force France to drink Coca-Cola, or abolish the French August vacation.

I had grown accustomed to the noise and the street music, and the shops and the kind of people I would never have met anywhere else. I was their token foreigner, and I was constantly being pointed out to visitors as their imperialist friend.

I went across the river and into the trees, where the students gathered, and found new lodging on the boulevard Montparnasse. It was a Polish cooperative called the Hôtel des États-Unis. The French had turned over the building to a group of Polish veterans who had fought with the allies in World War II.

It was conveniently located two blocks from the Dôme café, and La Rotonde, two of the leading intellectual cafés of Paris. Any evening one could share the sidewalk tables with Alexander Calder or Erskine Caldwell or Man Ray or Henry Miller — or so I was told by those who frequented the places.

All you had to do was sit, nursing a Pernod, and complain about the cultural excesses of the British and German literati. In the daytime, Montparnasse was just another *quartier,* but the area buzzed with activity in the evening. There were night clubs and restaurants, such as Jimmy's and Dominique, sucking up unsuspecting tourists.

Legend had it that in the thirties Hemingway had sat at Le Dôme, with a girl named Kiki. Now she was filled with wine and her face painted with terrible makeup. She went from café to café and danced on the tables while the crowd pretended to love it. I found it sad the first time I saw it — and even sadder each time after that. People in the know would whisper to visitors, "She was beautiful once and she belonged to Papa, so we still treat her with kindness."

The French café became my home away from home. There was no time limit on how long one could sit at a café table. French law forbade the waiter from whisking your glass away. Most of us started with white wine and asked for a bottle of soda water. As the drink got weaker, we kept pouring more soda into the glass until it was nothing but bubbly water.

French coffee was also one of the mainstays of our café lives. It was served as "filtre." Hot water was poured over coffee grounds, and in ten or fifteen minutes the coffee dripped into the cup. One of my early columns was titled "Garçon, my café won't filtre." It was about an ugly American who didn't have the patience to wait for the water to penetrate the coffee grounds.

Visitors to Paris sometimes asked which was the right row to occupy at the sidewalk café. I always told them that it was best to stay away from the first row, because you would be besieged by flower vendors and gypsies. The third row was too far back to truly observe the passing parade. So I recommended the second row, where you could still see everything and not be run over by a French driver looking for a parking space.

The cafés on the Champs-Elysées attracted a colorful mixture of tourists and hookers. For cover, the hookers usually had dogs with them. I never found out what happened to the dog when the hooker was entertaining a customer.

There was also an unwritten dress code for café-sitting, and it differed according to the location of the establishment. The Café de la Paix and the cafés on the Champs were favored by wealthy tourists, fashion models, and beautiful women on their way to Dior or Balenciaga. Consequently, everyone was elegant, with great legs. The Left Bank featured men in sweaters with ratty beards, and women with long, scraggly hair who, for the most part, wore neither makeup nor bras.

Choosing a café was like choosing a home. You knew that you would be returning again and again as long as you remained in Paris. Your social life revolved around the café of your choice. You left messages with the bartender, you began a love affair or ended one over a drink. Hours were spent rating poets and writers and speaking with contempt about any new writer who had become a success. Those who were politically inclined discussed how the U.S. was screwing up our foreign policy with the French. We never accused the French of screwing up their foreign policy, because we didn't know if they had one.

American students hung out in several sections of Paris. The three most popular were St-Michel, where the Sorbonne was located, St-Germain-des-Prés, and Montparnasse. St-Germain-des-Prés seated the vieux and nouveaux intellectuals, and had two wonderful cafés — the Café de Flore and the Café Les Deux Magots, which was patronized by those who worshipped at the feet of Jean-Paul Sartre and Simone de Beauvoir. They were also home to the *Paris Review* crowd, which included Alice B. Toklas, George Plimpton, Peter Matthiessen, James Baldwin, Richard

Wright, Bill Styron, Nancy Mitford, and William Burroughs.

Those who lived in Montparnasse looked down on the St-Germain-des-Prés crowd. We maintained that most of them were living off their grandmothers' trust funds. We viewed ourselves as the rightful heirs of D. H. Lawrence, Henry Miller, and Ford Madox Ford. We asserted forcefully that we did not have to sit next to Romain Gary or Gore Vidal to establish our literary credentials, like those in St-Germain.

Montparnasse even boasted an American women's dormitory off the boulevard, called Reid Hall, where young and innocent flowers from some of the most prestigious American universities were housed. Many fell in love with Frenchmen, but few American men fell in love with the American coeds. American men preferred to fall in love with French women, even if only to improve their language skills. The reasoning was that since they were in France for such a short period, it seemed wasteful to fall in love with an American girl. They could always do that when they got home to Baton Rouge.

In addition to the location, the price at the Hôtel was just right for me. I paid seven dollars a week for a room, including breakfast, which consisted of coffee and a sugared doughnut that made a tremendous thud when it hit the bottom of your stomach. The hotel rose seven stories. The entry on the ground floor was guarded by an ex-cavalry officer from Warsaw, who was now the commander in chief of mailboxes and keys. To the right was a bar-restaurant, which opened onto a sidewalk café. The bar came to life in the evening with a Hungarian piano player named Ernst, who had been imprisoned in a concentration camp. He doubled between a night club named Schubert's across the street and our bar, where he played for tips and vodka. Our place was popular and it was constantly filled with Americans and cigarette smoke. We had some strangers, but the majority were regulars from the neighborhood who wandered in and engaged in such varied activities as exchanging black-market money and negotiating liaisons of every sexual persuasion.

In the daytime, the students who were serious studied in the bar, while the ex-G.I.s who weren't sat nursing hang-overs, and eating a Warsaw version of a pork sausage and drinking a dark liquid, which the waiter claimed was coffee just like their mothers used to make.

You could be broke, studious, bombed, and sad in the bar — but you could never be lonely.

My room was on the third floor and looked out onto a brick wall of the next building. It had a sink, a bidet, a bed, a desk, and a light bulb so low in wattage that mice went blind trying to find something to eat. A maid vacuumed once a month and supplied one sheet and a weekly towel. If she gave us more than one towel, she was warned by the management that she would be shot by a Polish firing squad.

The sidewalk café of the hotel was small, but it had one interesting feature — it was located about fifty feet from an art-deco *pissoir*. The *pissoir* is one of France's most civilized monuments, for practical purposes more important than the Eiffel Tower. From our vantage point at the café, we could watch males of all shapes and sizes duck in to relieve themselves and then exit nervously. As we sat there, one of our games was to guess the profession of the person using the *pissoir,* based on the size of the instrument he was buttoning up. I recall one scene of a man readjusting his clothing as he was leaving, who bumped into a stylishly dressed woman. She screamed and, still clutching himself, the man tipped his hat with his other hand and bowed.

Everyone at the café applauded, and we divined he had to be a hotel concierge.

I patronized several restaurants in our neighborhood. My favorite was Henriette's, where I could get a full meal and wine for sixty-five cents. Wadja's was another. It served steaming platters of meat and potatoes at tables shared by all the patrons. At the end of the meal, I would confess to Madame Wadja what I had eaten, and she would tell me what I owed. I've dined at all the three-star restaurants in France, but the only place I get sentimental about is Wadja's. On my last visit to Paris, tears came to my eyes when I discovered that it was still open and that little had changed. The prices were low, the walls had never been painted, and another generation of students was hunched over the tables, digging into the piles of meat and vegetables. Madame Wadja had gone to heaven, but her daughter and her son carried on. In the forties, and fifties, Wadja's was one of the few restaurants that gave Americans much-needed nourishment at affordable prices.

The person we talked about the most was Ernest Hemingway. For aspiring writers in Paris, his name kept coming up, whether it was in connection with something he'd written or a bullfight someone had seen with him. He was the writer we all wanted to emulate — the man who exemplified the thirties and yet straddled life in Paris in the forties and fifties. What made him come alive for me was that Hemingway looked like Hemingway. None of the other writers of the period looked like who they were supposed to be, except possibly Gertrude Stein.

I knew Hemingway, yet I didn't know Hemingway. I met him through the circus owner John Ringling North, who used to hang out at the Ritz Bar. The first time I met God, he was bent over his drink. When we were introduced, my knees trembled and my hands shook. How does one behave in the presence of the Great One? It was too much for me to comprehend. I tried to remember all his books and was prepared to discuss them.

Then he said something which knocked me over. He said — and you will have to take my word for it — "Kid, have you ever wrestled a bear?"

I was dumbstruck. It was a perfect Hemingway question and one I still tell my grandchildren.

I replied, "What the hell?" But it didn't matter. With one bear-wrestling question, another one of my idols had become a mere mortal.

Some time after that, *Across the River and into the Trees* came out, and the book read like a parody of Hemingway. I wrote an article making fun of it. Years later, a friend showed me a letter he'd received from Hemingway, in which the Great One called me "a smart-assed son of a bitch."

I was very happy, because this meant he was reading me in the *Herald Tribune.*

Now, I don't want to put down Hemingway the writer. His work had a tremendous influence on me, as it did on all the writers of the thirties, forties, and fifties. Many of us studied his style, which was clean, poetic, and beautiful. The ones who made fools of themselves were those who, instead of studying his work, copied it and never developed a style of their own. Despite the fact that I never wrestled a bear, I am still his greatest fan. I have a first edition of his *A Moveable Feast*, given to me by his son, Jack, and I wish I could steal from it right now.

Papa (anyone who lived in Paris was allowed to call him Papa) inspired me in many ways. One time, when a friend of mine reported to me that he said to the Great One at a bullfight, "Mr. Hemingway, I want to be a writer — what do I do?" Hemingway replied, "First, you have to defrost the refrigerator."

When it came to bullfighting, we all emulated Papa's interest in the sport. In *Death in the Afternoon*, he wrote about a little old lady to whom he was explaining the intricacies of the sport. When I went to my first fight, I pretended that the little old lady had become a bloodthirsty aficionado, and had described the fight in graphic detail to me, a horrified novice.

Some of the established American writers living in Paris were nice to us younger ones. Thanks to Janet Flanner of *The New Yorker*, who lived in Paris and entertained everyone from the magazine, we got to know our heroes. Janet kept producing them in her suite at the Continental Hotel. People like E. B. White, James Thurber, S. J. Perelman, and A. J. Liebling. Each one of them had been someone I'd worshipped, and when I met them I always said something stupid, like, "Mr. Perelman, would you sign this book that I just bought at Brentano's? It's the British edition and much cheaper." Or, "Mr. White, how much money did you make writing *Charlotte's Web*?"

Jim Thurber, then blind, became a pal. Once I asked him what it was like to be blind. He replied, "It's better now. For a long while, images of Herbert Hoover were the only things that kept popping up in front of me."

Thurber was a menace in one respect. He was a smoker, and because of his blindness he kept putting out his cigarette on our furniture. I used to stand next to him with an ashtray, and when

45

he was ready to smash the cigarette out, I would place the ashtray in front of him like an outfielder with a baseball glove. I also knew and revered A. J. Liebling, who wrote about sports, the press, and food — not necessarily in that order. To me, it seemed that he knew everything about everything. He was especially easy to talk to.

Two of the funniest people in Paris in the early fifties were the poets Gregory Corso and Allen Ginsberg, who had founded the so-called "Beat Generation." They lived in a small hotel on the Left Bank — a hundred feet from the Seine.

Both claimed they had changed the course of poetry in America, Mr. Ginsberg at Columbia University and Corso in Dannemora Prison, where he had served three years for robbery.

"We measure our lines by breath — not beat," Ginsberg told me. "Edith Sitwell declared that the hope of English poetry is in America. We know she was right because she served us the best tea and watercress sandwiches we ever had."

Corso and I used to sit at a café on the Place St-Michel. One day, for no apparent reason, Corso said, "Give us poets time and we'll wrest the power from the priests."

"How do you get by?" I asked Corso.

"The foundations won't fund beat poets, so every time I meet a girl, I ask her how much money she has, and then I ask her for half. I'm not doing anything wrong with her money. I'm just using it to buy food."

A few weeks later, I went with both men to a reading at the Mistral Bookstore on the Left Bank. Forty or fifty people were in attendance. Another poet was reading his own work. Ginsberg was outraged, and yelled, "That isn't poetry." Someone yelled back, "What is your definition of poetry?"

Ginsberg stripped off all his clothes and recited his poems naked.

On that night, Ginsberg and Corso brought two Beat Generation bodyguards with them, who threatened to rough up anyone who tried to leave while Ginsberg was reading.

One time I ran into Corso, and he told me he had just had a fierce confrontation with Picasso.

"I asked him what he thought of

brown," Corso said. "Picasso thought I meant the color — but brown to me is biscuits which taste like sardines on the tongue of God. When I told him this, he hit me over the head with his hat. Then he hit me again. I knew from this reaction he would never give me a painting."

I said, "You should have asked for his hat."

One day in September 1948, I was walking through the lobby of the Crillon Hotel, when I bumped into a dapper little man with slicked-down hair and a moustache. He turned out to be a wild and crazy press agent called Guido Orlando from Cleveland, Ohio. A few weeks later, I discovered that he was the most audacious promoter I had ever come across. He wasn't in the business for the money, he was in it for the deal, the joy of conning clients, and snowing newspapermen.

The day I met him in the Crillon, he asked me what I was doing in Paris, and I told him that I was a student. He said, "Why don't you work for me?" I said okay. He then took me with him to talk to the hotel telephone operator.

He said to her, "Get me General de Gaulle." She was completely thrown off, but after several tries she got through to de Gaulle's headquarters. I heard Guido say to the person on the other end of the phone, "I hosted the General when he came to New York with Grover Whalen, and I have to see him right away. . . . No, I can't see him tomorrow, I have to see Churchill." He turned to me and said, "Let's go."

We went outside, and a limo was parked in front of the hotel. Guido said, "We'll take this." The chauffeur protested and explained that it was for the use of Mrs. Eleanor Roosevelt during her stay in Paris to attend a U.N. meeting. Guido ignored him, jumped in the back, and said, "Take me to General de Gaulle." I got in, and the chauffeur shrugged his shoulders and drove us away from the hotel. Guido said, "What shall I say to de Gaulle?" I replied, "Why don't you suggest that he write a book?" Guido was quiet for a few minutes, and then he said, "I think I'll suggest that he write a book."

We arrived at the General's HQ, and after explaining our mission, were ushered into the office of de Gaulle's secretary. Guido told her why it was imperative that he see the General, and took out some newspaper clippings. One had a photo of Guido with the Duke and Duchess of Windsor. They were all looking in different directions. Guido told the secretary that he really wanted to help de Gaulle save France from going Communist. He explained that he was confident this could be achieved through a good public relations campaign. I started to laugh and went off in the corner. The secretary looked at me, and said to Guido, "Can he be trusted?"

It turned out that de Gaulle wasn't in, and we finally left and got back in the limo. Guido said, "We still have an hour before lunch. What shall we do next?"

I kept running into Guido over the years in Paris. Every time I saw him, I thanked God that I hadn't gone to work for him!

Many years later, when I was working for the *Herald Tribune*, I finally got to meet General de Gaulle, without the help of Guido. I was invited to a white-tie reception in honor of President and Mrs. Kennedy.

We lined up in the grand hall, and

President Kennedy and General de Gaulle walked slowly down the line, shaking hands and talking to the guests. Kennedy was very slow and de Gaulle had to keep stopping to wait for him. I was standing in my place, when de Gaulle stopped in front of me and looked down and said in French, "Do you know all of the people in this room?"

I came to rigid attention, and squeaked, "Oui, mon général." De Gaulle nodded and walked on.

I remember being surprised at how very, very tall he was in real life, and when I was asked what de Gaulle was up to I would reply, "I don't know, but I'm up to the third button on his tunic."

The only other time I even came close to the General was when I attended a gala evening at the Paris Opera House in honor of Nikita Khrushchev, hosted by de Gaulle.

I walked out during the first act of the opera to scout the house and to see what was going on. On the second floor were heavy red drapes covering the windows that overlooked the Place de l'Opéra. I peered out, and there in the square were 20,000 boisterous members of the French Communist Party who had gathered to hail the Soviet leader.

I went out on the balcony and the crowd cheered. Then I waved my hand, and twenty thousand hands went up in response.

I made a fist and raised it again. Everyone's fist responded in kind. The crowd was going crazy.

I threw up both my arms. I'm certain there were a few in the crowd who were curious about my identity, but I was giving them something to do and they must have been grateful, as I appeared to be the only one who cared that they were standing there.

When the first act was over, I brought several friends out on the balcony, and together we waved and the crowd waved back. But I was sorry I had done it. I had felt so much power when I did it alone.

One of the joys of being an American in France was that you felt no responsibility for what happened there, as long as it did not interfere with the price of oysters. Strikes of every sort took place daily. No one suffered unless the bakers walked out. Some grievances were about public transportation — others involved the coal mines. The farmers kept dumping melons on the highways to protest low prices. I managed to survive several general strikes during which the entire country walked out. Since the French lifestyle was so precious, none of the strikes lasted very long. Consequently, everyone accepted them as part of the French way of life.

I lived through nineteen governments in fourteen years. They fell with regularity, as the different parties were clobbered in the elections and coalitions fell apart.

Everything seemed to run smoothly, sometimes more smoothly than when a specific party was actually in power.

This changed when Charles de Gaulle came to sit on the throne. All he had to do was go on radio and the whole country keeled over. "We are yours, mon général," they would say on their backs with their feet in the air. This is an exaggeration. De Gaulle was hated by the Left and feared by the Right. But France became slightly more stable under him, and the General could make the people do things other politicians couldn't.

One of the reasons that we paid so little attention to French domestic politics was that we were somehow convinced that if certain situations got too bad, the U.S. would send the Marines to save us.

Come to think of it, we weren't interested in American politics, either, although the Korean War did make us nervous. We were afraid they would find us in the Hôtel des États-Unis and ship us off to Asia.

Almost anybody who would become anybody came to Paris in the fifties. One student at the time was Robert Redford. I didn't know about this until he told me his story when he was making *All the President's Men.*

"I had been a very lonely art student in Paris. One day," he told me, "I found the Bar l'Abbaye, a tiny place around the corner from St-Germain-des-Prés where two American folk singers, Lee Payant and Gordon Heath, entertained. After several evenings, Lee and Gordon invited me backstage, and every night after that between shows I spent time with them. Then I went home and started working in movies. I didn't come back for seven years. I dreamed of returning to the Bar l'Abbaye. I walked in around ten o'clock and sat there with a grin on my face. I waved, and Gordon nodded at me. I finally said, 'Hey, Gordon, Lee, don't you know who I am?'

" 'Sure,' Gordon said, 'you're the actor Robert Redford,' " Redford told me sadly. "They didn't know who I was!"

There were always hijinks at the Hôtel des États-Unis. Once, Raleigh Peters, an impecunious sometime Sorbonne student, took a hooker up to his room for the night. When it came time to pay, he called the desk and said, "I have a lady friend here, and when she comes down, please give her five thousand francs. What do you mean the safe is locked and you can't open it? What kind of hotel do you people run?" He told the angry lady to come back the next day for her money. She did return, with two burly Corsicans, who asked to see Raleigh personally. The man at the front desk sized up the situation, and told them that Raleigh had left that morning for Korea. He counted out the money owed the girl as fast as he could. One of the escorts said, "Tell him, if he ever talks to one of our ladies again, we will put his chestnuts in your safe and close the door very hard on them."

A worldwide event took place at the Hôtel des États-Unis in 1948. One of the roomers there was Garry Davis, the son of Meyer Davis, the society band-leader. Garry was an idealist and wanted to start a world government, to replace all the faulty ones then in ex-istence. To dramatize this, he decided to become the first World Citizen by giving up his American passport in front of the Palais de Chaillot where the U.N. was meeting. After World War II, an American passport was the most cherished document on earth. Anybody who would give one up was regarded as crazy. The plans for the passport sur-render were formulated in the bar of the Hôtel des États-Unis. We weighed the pros and cons of Garry's act. If he did it, we warned him, the French would arrest him for not having proof he ex-isted. Garry said that was exactly what he had in mind. He wanted to prove how ridiculous any sort of identification papers really were.

Since there wasn't much going on that day, we encouraged him to do it.

The news traveled fast and Mrs. Eleanor Roosevelt called Garry and tried to discourage him from following through on his plan. She pointed out that it would look bad for the United States if someone tore up his passport at a U.N. meeting. But Garry had made his mind up, and the next morning he went down to the Palais de Chaillot and tore it into pieces. The police arrested him for not having proper identification.

A star was born. Every paper headlined the story. It was wonderful theater. Clad in his leather bomber jacket, Garry became a hero and an instant celebrity. For fifteen minutes, people were transfixed by the idea of World Citizenship. They didn't like it enough to give up their own passports — but they celebrated the courage of Davis turning in his.

We were the beneficiaries of Garry's noble deed. The Hôtel des États-Unis was suddenly besieged by foreign correspondents and newsreel cameramen. I volunteered assessments on Garry to anyone who offered to buy me a drink.

I spoke with authority. "Yes, Garry always marched to a different drummer, even though he never owned a drum. He is a visionary — a man who would slide out on the wing of a plane to see how much ice was on it. Garry told us in this very bar how sick and tired of war and rumors of war he was. He feels that his lack of a passport will bring the major powers to their senses again."

Or I said, "I always thought of Garry as Jesus Christ without a tourist visa. Someday, when there is only one world and the capital of it is Montparnasse, people will visit this hotel as if it were a shrine and light a candle at the *pissoir* out in front."

I predicted to the press that the Hôtel would be regarded as the equivalent of the train that had taken Lenin to St. Petersburg.

The initial notoriety was exciting. But things got complicated when Garry was released from jail. He announced that he was making the Hôtel des États-Unis headquarters for the World Citizenship movement. Suddenly, paperless exiles carrying sleeping bags began to show up at the hotel. They were all stateless and they felt that Garry was their last hope. But as soon as they appeared, so did the French police, who rounded everyone up because they had no passports or identification cards.

The Black Marias made a run to the hotel on the hour.

We also entertained a scruffy bunch of undercover agents from assorted major and minor powers. They were trying to figure out what country was behind Garry and how to turn his movement into a profitable intelligence investment.

It is a well-known fact that the forties and fifties were golden years for all the spooks. They had money to burn for recruiting people to do their dirty work for them. From *The Third Man*, as played by Orson Welles, to the Kim Philby defection, everyone was intent on getting inside information from the other side. If nothing else, it made John le Carré an extremely rich man.

The CIA was very much open for business in Europe — and one of its schemes was to recruit students as observers and infiltrators. The students were not asked to rub out a KGB competitor but rather to infiltrate left-wing student groups and report back. Years later, some of our most distinguished liberal citizens admitted to taking money and plane tickets from the CIA during that time.

One day in the late seventies, I was walking down Fifth Avenue, and I ran into an acquaintance from the Paris days. "You know," I said, "when you and I lived at the Hôtel des États-Unis, I always thought that you worked for the CIA."

"Isn't that funny," he replied. "I always thought you did."

I was never considered a possible recruit, but over the years I had run-ins with the CIA. Once, I went to Karlovy Vary in Czechoslovakia for a film festival. It had been a famous spa for the aristocracy, and then when Communism took over, it became a favored vacation place for the workers. Over the post-war years, the buildings had deteriorated, but the Czechs still came there for baths.

After returning to Paris and writing several columns about it, I was visited by two stern men in dark suits, who said they wanted to talk to me about the Czech film festival.

"Yes," I said.

"How many Russian tanks did you see

between Prague and Karlovy Vary?" one asked me.

"I slept most of the way in the car."

"Did you notice any anti-aircraft guns around the film festival hall?"

"Hey, I thought you guys wanted to know about films."

One of them pulled out a CIA identity card. "We would feel better if you answered our questions without any lip."

This ticked me off. "If you really want to know what I saw in Czechoslovakia, why don't you take two francs and buy the *Herald Tribune*?"

They felt insulted and stood up. I thought this would mark me as a traitor with the agency for life. But it was not so. Years later, when I was living in Washington, I asked for my CIA folder, which I was permitted to have under the Freedom of Information Act. There was a lot of junk — mostly clippings from the paper of a trip I had taken to the Soviet Union — but nothing about the visit of the two men. I wrote back and told them their file was incomplete, since it said nothing about the CIA agents I had kicked out of my office.

Two curious events did occur in Czechoslovakia, though, that I didn't tell the CIA about. The giant dining hall at the spa had tables for each nationality, decorated with the country's flag. There were only two Americans present — Gene Moscowitz from *Variety* and myself. For a short while, I had been the Paris stringer on the show-business paper, and Gene had succeeded me. I had told Gene at the time that he should use the job to get a decent position in the motion-picture business. He'd agreed, but instead remained with *Variety* for the rest of his life. In thirty years, he never missed an international film festival.

Our table was very long and could seat at least twenty. Because of our numbers, everyone was curious about the "American delegation" and kept looking at us and whispering to each other. After the first evening, I said to Moscowitz, "Let's give them something to whisper about. At lunch you sit at one end of the table and I'll sit at the other, and we won't talk to each other."

We did just that the next day. We were separated by a mile of table cloth and did not even look at each other. We kept it up at every meal, and the dining room was buzzing for two days. They were certain we had had a bitter fight, but they weren't sure what it was about.

We continued the charade until a kid named Robert Keller showed up wearing a Miami U. sweatshirt and driving a beat-up Volkswagen. We asked him what interest he had in films. He said, "None, I just came to take my driver's test. I've flunked it in every country in Western Europe, so I figure this might be a good place to pass it."

That afternoon, driving the only car on the road, Keller took his test and passed it with flying colors. The next morning, he blew town without paying his hotel bill, and Moscowitz and I had to convince the management that we had never met him before.

We had lost all interest in the way the Davis movement was going at the hotel, when one day we found a notice in our mail boxes. It was a terse letter from the management, announcing that Garry planned to take over all the rooms in the hotel for the administration of his World Citizenship movement.

The residents agreed that it was a bunch of pork sausage, and we announced we were not going to leave for some crazy peace movement. The tenants informed the Poles that we would not be moved.

For two weeks, there was a standoff between the Hôtel management and ourselves. We refused to accept the eviction notices.

Then something happened which made them change their minds. Garry's people couldn't come up with the rent. Despite the heavy volume of mail that kept arriving, no envelopes contained any money. When Garry failed to pay his rent, the management started to worry about us leaving. They told Garry that unless he paid up, his movement was out on the street. For several weeks, in order not to lose us, the Poles treated us with the respect we thought ex-American G.I.s deserved.

The movement as a movement died, but through the years Garry has stuck to his guns. He has been thrown in jail in every country he has entered because he has tried to use his World Passport as a legal document. Today, Garry wanders alone from newspaper office to newspaper office, handing out press releases. And he's always upbeat. Garry Davis gave us an exciting time during our student days in Paris, and he shall always be remembered by those who were witness to his grand gesture. His vision of world government was slightly premature, but some of it actually is happening. Look at the European Union, and other alliances that are not only financial but political successes. Europeans are no longer required to carry passports to visit one another. I pray that someday the Hôtel des États-Unis will be renamed the Garry Davis Ritz.

Things were rolling along in Paris. The Marshall Plan had been inaugurated by Harry Truman, and its headquarters were established in the French capital. The Plan had several purposes — one was to get Europe back on its feet and another was to keep the Western half from going Communist. The plan worked by giving goods to the Europeans, as well as by providing skills that were badly needed at the time. Averell Harriman headed the operation and he attracted outstanding people from all walks of life.

These had to be legally supplemented by Americans — like the G.I. playboys who hung out at the Hôtel des États-Unis. The best part of the Marshall Plan was that no one remained in his or her position for long. George Anderson, a buddy from USC, applied for a job as a mimeograph operator and wound up printing all the money in France, or so he maintained. The rest of the Hôtel residents were quickly promoted to such jobs as instructing the Italians on how to make pasta, the Danes on how to make cheese, and the Benelux countries on how to run their coal and steel industries. The truth was that my friends were more interested in the American PX privileges than they were in saving Europe.

I applied for a job as a mimeograph operator, but there was a lady in personnel named Marion Foley who just didn't believe I had what it took to turn a wheel on a machine and duplicate official papers.

"Let me start out cleaning the ink off the drum," I begged.

She said she couldn't take a chance. All the Western powers were involved with the Marshall Plan — one bad duplication and the alliance could fall apart.

"Then let me do something else. I could teach the Belgians how to make lace or the Dutch how to repair windmills."

Marion wanted no part of me, and she pointed to the door.

I was distraught, but she was right. Now I get down on my knees every night and bless the sainted Marion Foley. Had she given me a government job, I would now be in a retirement home in Sun City dreaming of my triumphs in Paris with my mimeograph machine.

The Marshall Plan was one of the most successful financial and diplomatic adventures in which the United States ever engaged. Since it came so swiftly and with such good feeling, the recipients were suspicious that there were strings attached. What worried the countries most was that no one was asking for a payoff in exchange for the aid.

The longer there was no extortion, the more nervous everyone became. Suddenly into this vacuum stepped Jim Nolan, who was an advertising manager at the *Herald Tribune.* Jim went to the

Italians and said he was from the *Trib* and he would like to print an entire supplement, with ads, of course, extolling the virtues of Italian industry and culture. The Italian government officers were overjoyed. One shouted, "Thank God, the payoff."

Jim was so successful with the Italians wanting to give something back that he made the rounds of the other Marshall Plan countries. No one dared refuse, and all felt they could sleep better at night knowing that they had finally paid off someone for the U.S. dollars.

When the Marshall Plan rejected me, I got a job as a stringer for the American show-business journal, *Variety*. I was introduced to a seventy-five-year-old Frenchman named Max de Beix, who was a *Variety* stringer himself. I talked myself into being *his* stringer. It paid nothing, but it gave me entrée into all the show-business enterprises, including movies and vaudeville. It also gave me a chance to attend fancy cocktail parties where I served myself dinner. Max didn't care what I did, as long as I kept handing him stories he could file to New York.

He was a fascinating man. His real name was Levy, and he was sixty-five when the Germans marched into Paris. To save him, a family named de Beix had adopted him and he'd taken their name. Max knew everyone in show business in Paris. His dispatches to New York were read and taken seriously, but he was getting on in years and he did not mind having someone to help him.

The fact that I had a job did not make me too popular with my friends at the Hôtel. I could feel the hostility.

One Saturday afternoon, I was sitting in the bar with Phil George, Art Kaplan, George Penty, and Jerry Conrad, when I was called to the phone. The conversation went something like this:

"Mr. Buchwald, this is Billy Rose. I'm here with my wife, Eleanor, and Abel Green [the editor of *Variety*] said that you would show us the town."

I smelled a rat. "Well, eff you, Mr. Rose, and eff Eleanor as well." And I hung up. I returned to the table and said, "Nice work, guys, but I didn't bite."

They had no idea what I was talking about, because it *was* Billy Rose, the impresario. The funny part of the story is that Billy Rose had so many enemies, he spent the rest of his time in Europe trying to remember what he had done to me to elicit such an angry response.

Later, Abel Green sent me a steaming letter telling me that if I ever did something like that again, I was going to have my head and legs chopped off.

All the time I was working for *Variety* as a stringer, my eye was on the *Herald Tribune.* Every young journalist's dream was to work on the *Trib.* As far as I know, it still is. Europe being Europe, most newspapers were either owned by or in debt to a political party. The *Trib* was an American paper with no ax to grind, and the readers trusted it. This, by the way, has not changed. Every day, it was distributed throughout nineteen countries on the Continent, and it was the American tourist's lifeline to home.

The European edition of the *New York Herald* was founded in October 1887 by a wealthy eccentric from New York named James Gordon Bennett. The story goes that Bennett, the son of the New York paper's owner, was something of a playboy. One night, at a fancy Long Island party honoring his engagement to the beautiful Caroline May,

Bennett took a leak in the ballroom piano. (Some say he urinated in the living-room fireplace, but the piano makes a better story.) This caused quite a scandal in his social circle. The engagement was broken, and Caroline's brother horsewhipped Bennett on the steps of the Union Club. (This information comes from Charles Robertson, whose history, *The International Herald Tribune — The First Hundred Years,* is the best written about the paper.)

Bennett challenged May to an illegal duel, but neither man drew blood. Banished from New York society, Bennett left for Paris, where he lived for the next forty years. Rumor has it that he made his decision to stay when he heard the hooting of an owl in the Bois de Boulogne. It was said that he loved owls, and therefore considered what he heard to be an omen. I make it a practice to believe every story I have ever heard about the *Herald Tribune,* so I believe the piano, the duel, and the owl.

Once Bennett started his paper, he introduced all sorts of wireless communications, which put his paper on top of the news and attracted readers who wanted to know what was going on in the United States. He also mixed it with gossip of the International Set, which attracted European readers. He was filthy rich, and owned houses and palaces all over Europe, as well as luxurious yachts: one called the *Lysistrata* had a crew of one hundred.

Apparently, Bennett was not a nice man when he was drunk. He had a bad temper and was exceedingly cruel to people who couldn't fight back. He was also very harsh to those who worked on the *Trib*. He fired people on a whim. One day a staffer was in good favor, the next he'd be out on the street. It was amazing how, with all his contempt for journalists, he was able to put out such an incredible publication.

I yearned to work on the paper more than anything I had ever wanted in my life. But how? As I studied the *Trib,* it dawned on me that it had no entertainment column, and yet Paris was the entertainment capital of the world. Tourists always wanted to know where to go, and I was prepared to lead them. I hoped that my *Variety* experience would give me an inside track, though I was prepared to lie about everything else, including my credentials, my education, and my ability to speak foreign languages.

I set off to try my luck.

Chapter 3

The *Trib*

I went to see Eric Hawkins, the managing editor, and asked him if I could cover Paris night life, since I had been doing it for *Variety.*

Eric was a feisty Englishman who had been a boxer before he became a newspaperman. He ran the paper for thirty years and seemed to be the only one in management who knew how to put it out. He was rumored to be a ladies' man, though I never saw this side of him myself. In the beginning, he and I had problems — mainly because I had no experience and he didn't like the idea of me using the *Tribune* to get some.

After listening to my story, and signing his mail at the same time, he said, "The paper isn't interested in an entertainment column, and if it was, you wouldn't be the one to write it. Now get the hell out of here."

Some people would consider this a rejection. I didn't. A few weeks later, I heard that Eric had returned to England on home leave, so I went back to the paper and asked to speak to the editor, Geoff Parsons. I said, "Mr. Hawkins and I have been talking about me doing an entertainment column." I think that I also said something about the column generating more advertising. I had uttered the magic word. Parsons' eyes lit up, and he hired me for $25 a week to write two columns — one on films and one on night clubs.

I couldn't believe it. Without any demand to see my credentials, or even questioning my writing ability, Parsons had changed my life. I was on the staff of the greatest newspaper in the greatest city in the world, and I would get $25 a week for the rest of my life.

I never knew James Gordon Bennett, but I owe him a debt. Had he not peed in a piano and founded the *Herald*, I might not have been sitting at a desk in the city room smoking a cigar with a big grin on my face when Eric Hawkins returned from England and found me. It took him weeks to get over seeing me there.

The fact that I had gone over his head and wound up on the paper was an affront to his authority. In time, he got over the fact I had done an end run around him, and we became good friends, so much so that when he was forced to retire, I talked him into writing his memoirs and found a publisher for him. In exchange, I came out very well in his book.

I discovered that I was not the first saloon writer ever to grace the *Trib*. Before World War II, in the twenties and thirties, a diminutive sixty-year-old man, sporting a fedora hat, had held the title. His name had been Sparrow Robertson, and he'd written what he called "sporting gossip" but was really a daily collection of names he had run into in various bars — the most pre-eminent of which was Harry's New York Bar on rue Daunou. He had a large readership, and although he had covered sports, his fame had grown when he kept listing everyone he ran into as "my old pal." He'd been everyone's drinking companion, and would stay up all night with tourists on a "death watch" before pouring them on the boat train back to the U.S.

Sparrow had remained in Paris for a year after the German occupation and passed away in his eighties. I never knew him, but since his name kept popping up over the years, I would have liked to have spent at least an afternoon with him.

At the beginning, I had to pinch myself to believe I was part of the *Trib* staff. For one thing, there were so few of us. For another, the *New York Herald Tribune* in New York favored Ivy League journalists. It was as if I had climbed over the fence of Yankee Stadium and wound up sitting on the bench with Joe DiMaggio.

I'd always loved to write, but I had no idea what kind of writer I wanted to be. I liked the idea of writing for films, because it paid well and I would get to live in Hollywood. What I didn't realize was that writers count for nothing in the movie business, and while they are paid thousands of dollars to produce a script, people could care less about their work.

Playwriting appealed to me, too. I had taken a course at USC and I loved dialogue. I also had written the annual USC varsity show *No Love Atoll,* but you have to starve writing for the stage before you become successful at it and see your name on Broadway. Years later, when I lived in Washington, I wrote a play called *Sheep on the Runway.* It made it to the Great White Way, and seeing my name on the marquee was a memorable moment for me. The show didn't stay too long, but the reviews were fine, and I thought that playwriting was an honorable profession, unlike movie-writing, because on Broadway no one could change a word without the writer's permission.

And then there was newspaper-writing. I did not want to be a straight reporter. I preferred feature-writing, as I had done in the Marine Corps, where I'd mixed fantasy and facts in the same story, or the kind of column I'd written for the *Daily Trojan,* in which I'd invented my own sorority, the "O Mi Gods," and devoted the space to making fun of the Greek system.

Neither my grammar nor spelling was very good, but the ideas kept pouring out and could carry the story. If I had applied for a job on a paper in New York without a college degree, I would have been bounced out on my ear.

Even though I've been in the business for over forty-six years, I still don't really see myself as a "writer." I have worked on newspapers all my professional life, but I don't really consider myself a "journalist," mainly because I invented most of the material for my columns. Sometimes I have settled for the designation of "columnist," but with the exception of Russell Baker, Dave Barry, or Art Hoppe, the "columnist" label never quite fit the humor category.

I think I have avoided the term "writer," because I had always been in awe of the writers I have personally known. I am talking now of people like Bill Styron, Irwin Shaw, John Hersey, Lillian Hellman, Joe Heller, and Mary McCarthy. They have the ability to put thousands of words together to weave tales that hold your attention with emotion and ideas.

My column has never been longer than six hundred words. The articles comprise a beginning, a middle, and an end. My craft is more sketching than writing; my column is almost a cartoon in words.

But I have gained satisfaction from the fact that the most talented writers of our time could not write a six-hundred-word column. When I used to go on vacation, I would ask John Steinbeck, or Irwin Shaw, or even Vladimir Nabokov to fill in as guest columnists. They did, but they found the length restriction all but impossible. They gave it their best shot but then realized that writing lengthy pieces was much easier.

All of my luck in writing since has been the result of my landing that job on the *Trib* in Paris. I doubt that I could have gotten away with my kind of articles for a newspaper in the United States. The *Trib* had a unique audience and, luckily for me, the paper had editors like Geoff Parsons and Eric Hawkins who let me have my way.

The *Herald Tribune* offices were located at 21, rue de Berri, off the Champs-Elysées. Across the street was the California Hotel, whose bar we frequented before, during, and after work. Down toward the Champs was a tiny hotel called the Lancaster, where Elizabeth Taylor, Audrey Hepburn, and John Huston used to stay. Next to it was the

Hungarian Embassy, its shutters closed at all times. The rumor among the *Trib* staff was that they tortured people in their basement and sent their heads back to Budapest in diplomatic pouches. And next to the paper was a night club called L'Aiglon, where we also went after work.

The *Tribune,* alas, has since moved out of the center of Paris, to a section in an ugly part of Neuilly, and is now housed in a grim steel building amongst other unappealing buildings. It is much easier to put out the paper there, and there is more desk room for the staff. But anyone who worked on the rue de Berri thinks of the present building as a pile of nouveau junk.

The editorial room in the old building, where my desk was located, could not have been better designed by a movie-set director. The floors sagged, and when the presses were running, the entire building shook. The furniture was a mixture of pre-war and early post-war flotsam, and you never knew when a chair or a desk would collapse on you. The limited space allotted to me could have gotten the *Tribune* in trouble with the Geneva Convention.

My desk, a brown, dingy piece of furniture, was perpendicular to the wall. As I sat at my typewriter, I faced a blind window which overlooked a soot-covered air shaft.

To my left, no more than eight feet away, was an oval table which served as the copy desk. Eight people worked at the desk — some editing stories and others writing headlines.

Behind this desk was a shaft which went down to the composing room. The copy was dropped in it, where it was set by French printers who, because they didn't know English, rarely made a mistake when transcribing it.

Besides producing the newspaper, the printers also provided the music in the building. Every twenty minutes, the strains of the *Internationale* wafted up the shaft and flooded the office. Although it was the Communist anthem, Americans in the editorial room all joined in. This was just one of the things that made the *Herald Tribune* such a special place to work. Where else could Communists and Americans sing together?

Something that really bothered me was that everyone was constantly reading my mail, which was all over the desk top. The night shift also used my desk as a table for carry-out lasagna dinners. In the morning when I came in, I had to clear away whatever they had eaten the night before.

I particularly remember the man in charge of the mail, who wore thick, tinted glasses, and as far as I know was legally blind. He brought each letter up to his face, studied it, and then put it in the wrong box anyway.

The telephone operator was deaf. She could hear people talking on the phone, but she could not hear the bells ringing on the board. Since there were faulty lights all the time, we were in constant trouble.

One of the biggest safety hazards was the toilet seat in the men's room, which had a serious crack. No matter how you sat you got painfully pinched by it.

Some of the best writing I did on the *Trib* was the memos I wrote to everyone about the seat, from the Reid family in New York to Jock Whitney, who was then ambassador to Great Britain and had acquired the *Trib*.

"How can you expect to put out a newspaper," I pleaded with the powers

that be, "when every time your reporters sit down in the men's room, they
scream in agony? This seat, installed
during the early days of World War One,
has given pain to generations of journalists. The *Herald Tribune,* which
fights against all forms of torture, is
committing its own by not replacing the
cracked throne. We are not asking for
new presses or even new typewriters,
though God knows we need both. But
it is our asses we are fighting for, and
management has a duty to preserve
them if they want to continue to publish
a fine newspaper.

"How would Ambassador Whitney like
to work on this paper and then have to
go across the street to the California
Hotel to avoid his precious diplomatic
bottom being pinched?"

The letters marked me as a possible
union organizer.

Every available inch of space was
used in the editorial room. The sports
editor was seated across from me. He
was a free spirit, and his technique was
to promise to marry every woman he
bedded down with. He was certain
French red tape would save him. It did,
until one day, when he went down to

the city hall with a lady friend to go through the motions of getting the proper papers. Instead of refusing them, the lady behind the counter said she would let nothing stand in the way of love, and it didn't matter if his credentials were good or not, he could get married.

The sports editor wasn't as much fun to work with after that.

The copy desk was manned by a kindly soul named Roy McMullen, who put up with the bad copy I was writing. He was surrounded by desk men who wrote headlines. To their left was the City Desk, composed of three reporters, Jim Knight, Bob Haney, and Bob Yoakum. In the corner sat the travel editor, first Paul Ress and then Bob Sage. The majority of the copy for the travel page was releases written by press agents employed to beat the drum for their countries and their resorts. It's possible there were some unfavorable reviews of travel places that advertised in the paper, but I can't recall one. We had an unwritten law: Never knock a country that feeds you.

In the back was the library, with large bound compilations of the *Trib* sagging on the shelves. The librarians changed constantly, but the archives were a gold mine of information covering seventy-five years of American life in Paris. It was used by scholars writing books (mostly on U.S. presidents and American politics), by lawyers looking for evidence to help their clients collect inheritances, and by students who just wanted to keep warm in the winter.

Our salaries were sufficient, and New York was very pleased with our profits. The reason we were doing so well was that the general manager of the paper forgot to pay French social security taxes. When the French discovered this, all hell broke loose and the paper was fined zillions of francs. New York blamed everyone on the editorial staff for this blunder, in spite of the fact that we never saw a nickel of their money. We had to assure each accountant the *Trib* sent over from New York that we had had nothing to do with French social security money, and they could body-search us if they doubted it.

I did not have an auspicious start as a columnist, and there was good reason to fire me after several columns. I tried to be Walter Winchell, Ed Sullivan, and

H. L. Mencken all in one.

A few years later, Eric Hawkins told a *Newsweek* reporter, "He wasn't exactly a whirlwind in the beginning. In fact, his copy was impossible. He was a complete novice at writing. He had the ideas, but he didn't know what to do with them. Also, his bad French didn't help. I remember some of his first pieces consisted of rewriting menus. When he wrote about the cinema, a typical Buchwald review in those days might wind up with the comment, 'This is a good film if you understand French.'"

(I had solved the problem of how to review films with my faulty French by giving every French picture, no matter how bad, a good notice. I assumed no French producer would question my language credentials if I praised his picture. I was right.)

Hawkins continued, "But his naïveté served him well. Gradually, he developed an identification with almost every American tourist in Paris. He was constantly fighting waiters or being baffled by wine lists. He became the typical bumbling American in Paris."

Everyone must have a rabbi to succeed in his career. I had many — Eric Hawkins, Frank Dorsey, Roy McMullen, Geoff Parsons, and Dick Wald all come to mind. I'm sure there were others. All of these people flinched when I handed in my copy in the early days, and although most are no longer with us, I owe my career to their patience and understanding.

I knew I wasn't doing well, and I was prepared for the ax to fall at any moment. It was a fearful thought, since I had told everyone I knew back home that I was a columnist on the Paris *Trib.* I wasn't sure how well I could handle the disgrace of being canned, so I reacted the only way I knew how: The realization that my days were numbered made me have some fun. Instead of emulating the Broadway columnists, I started writing in my own style — I cast myself as a Charlie Chaplin character in my column, the hapless tourist who couldn't shoot straight.

People started talking about it — and I was off and running. The ever-patient Eric Hawkins encouraged me to remain in this groove.

As the new boy in town, I did certain things that my fellow workers found revolting. One was that I chain-smoked cigars, and there was no fresh air in the city room to absorb the smoke. Then I found that I'd burst out laughing at my own stuff as I was typing it. Nobody really cared for that. Finally, I decorated my wall with a giant-sized poster that I had bought in East Berlin of Joseph Stalin with his arm raised. I tied a Coca-Cola bottle from the ceiling, and it looked as if Stalin was drinking a Coke. It was a nice work of art, but it shook up visiting brass from New York. When they came to the city room, they saw Stalin, but they missed the Coke bottle. After only one such visit from Helen Reid, Eric made me take it down.

The staff hated the poster, but once the *Trib*'s owners said they did too, they agreed it was as gripping as a Matisse.

One day, we got word that Jock Whitney would pay a visit to Paris and the paper. This announcement was followed by futile attempts to clean the city room. It was impossible, since there was no place to deposit the dust which had gathered over the years. The desks were cleared and we stuffed years of yellowed press releases in the drawers and in the file cabinets in the library.

Eric warned me to behave myself and not to bring up the subject of the cracked toilet seat.

"Why not?" I asked.

"Because," he replied, "we told Whitney that we're working on the problem."

When word got out that Whitney was in the building, we all lined up like good soldiers to be reviewed. Whitney passed us, shaking hands with each one of us as we told him what we did.

Count Alain De Lyrot, a reporter, did everything but kiss Whitney on the lips. When the ambassador departed, Ursula Naccache, my secretary, accused De Lyrot of sucking up to the new owner.

De Lyrot defended his action by saying, "If my ancestors hadn't kissed the king's ass hundreds of years ago, I wouldn't be a count today."

Not long after this visit, Eric moved me upstairs to my own office on the third floor, leaving me to smoke and laugh alone. I furnished it with a BarcaLounger I imported from the United States.

I had a very difficult time getting it through customs. Ursula went down to fight for me. She explained to the *douane* that I had a very bad back from fighting with the Free French in World War II, and that this was the only chair the doctors recommended. She pleaded and cajoled — two of her major suits — and we managed to get it into the country for free.

I would not have traded my Barca for a Louis XVI chaise longue. It was the only comfortable chair in the *Trib* office, so I sat in it, legs stretched out, putting visitors at a certain disadvantage. I recall a stuffy U.S. senator stopping by and becoming very nervous because he had to look at the soles of my shoes. What really pissed him off, he told the American ambassador, was when I said, "Forgive me for not getting up."

The *Tribune* was good to me, and as I progressed, they permitted me to hire secretaries, first Jo Patrick, then Roni Herr, then Sue Graham, and finally Ursula Naccache. They were all loving and efficient, and I was devoted to them, particularly when they took my side with French bureaucrats about my personal problems.

Tragedy struck Roni Herr, a quiet Smith College graduate. Roni owned a Renault 4CV, which could be blown off any bridge on a windy night, and one day she told me she was going to take a two-week vacation in Spain with a young male acquaintance — a poet.

A few days into the trip, I was notified by the U.S. Embassy in Madrid that a truck had crashed into her car and smashed it to bits, and that both Roni and her companion had been killed.

I called her parents in the United States. Her mother asked me if I could arrange to have Roni's remains shipped back home to New England. I said I would.

But I was soon to discover that it was next to impossible to get a deceased person out of Spain. The paperwork was enormous. To make matters even worse, the Spanish wanted me to pay $700 in customs duties on Roni's car, which had been crushed to bits by a Spanish truck driver. I wrote back that I would send a check, but the body had to be returned immediately. Eventually we did manage to get Roni and the poet home. But I never sent the check to Spanish customs. As soon as Roni was out of the country, I suggested they give the car to Franco instead.

Once Roni was buried, I began the job of haggling with the Spanish insurance company. From police reports, it was obvious that the truck that had killed her was definitely at fault. I was hoping to get some money for the family, not only for Roni but for the young man.

The company played hardball. In the end, I wound up with very little insurance money for Roni and less for the poet. The company told me that Roni had had no future as a secretary, so did not merit a generous settlement, and they didn't even list poets as a legitimate profession — so his life was worth nothing. Recently, I asked an insurance friend how much a poet's life was worth in America, and he said no more than it was in Spain.

Ursula, dear Ursula, was not only my secretary, she pitied me and was determined to protect me from the French authorities. Without her, I'm sure I would have wound up on Devil's Island, or in Algeria with the French Foreign Legion.

Although Swiss, she yelled over the phone like a wounded French housewife. Or she purred like Brigitte Bardot, when it was appropriate. The battles she fought for me with authorities included ones over taxes, identity cards for work permits, my children's adoption papers, and French red tape of every kind.

Once, a French IRS man came into the office and said that I owed him the equivalent of $300, which was a surtax on something or other. I discussed it with Ursula, and she whispered, "Pay it, and you are going to see something funny."

I started writing out a check, when the agent said, "Aren't you going to protest it?"

I said I wasn't, because I lived in France and believed that I should pay my fair share of taxes.

"But everyone is protesting this tax. If I bring back your check, my superior will want to know why I haven't collected from the others."

Ursula chimed in, "Do you want his money or not?"

"No," he said in anger, and walked out of the office.

Ursula had her own red-tape problems, which produced several columns. She wanted to marry a French doctor. Since she was a foreigner, the authorities had to grant permission if the ceremony took place in France, but the prune-faced bureaucrats kept finding errors in her papers.

Finally I came up with an idea for her. I suggested that Ursula hide a scarf under her dress to make her look pregnant and go back to the bureau. She did. As she pointed to her stomach, she sobbed, "I have to get married."

The lady looked down, shook her head, and said, "It's not serious enough yet."

I made her go back two weeks later with three scarves under her dress. This time the woman said, "Now it's serious."

Being pregnant in France had its just rewards. As a woman with child, Ursula was treated with tremendous respect. When she visited the welfare bureau, someone immediately brought her a chair. Then a social security supervisor came out from his office to congratulate her. All the people behind a counter filling out papers smiled and talked very softly.

One of them gave her a list of medical tests she was required to take, which of course would be paid for by the French government.

Someone informed her that she would

also receive $40 for each medical visit, and when the baby was born, an additional $80.

Then she was handed a Carte de Priorité, which was carried by war invalids, blind people, and pregnant women. This card entitled Ursula to a seat on the subway, and the right to get up front in the bus line. She did not have to stand in line in post offices, railroad stations, and automobile shows. Department stores also gave priority.

When Ursula returned, she showed me the *carte* and said, "When French drivers see a pregnant woman crossing the street, they have to stop, even if they don't want to."

"You're not going to test that one?" I said.

She laughed. "Not on your life."

In the late forties and fifties, the *Trib* covered Paris much more heavily than it did the rest of Europe. The theater critic was Thomas Quinn Curtiss. Lucie Noel and Hebe Dorsey wrote mainly about Paris fashions, and I reviewed French restaurants. Our three reporters covered French news. This caused fights between the editorial and circulation departments, as well as the people in advertising, who maintained that the rest of the Continent was being ignored.

There was probably some truth to this, but our readership was so scattered over the nineteen countries, and the only town in which the tourists and American residents were concentrated was Paris. I was given leeway to travel anywhere, and so I covered Rome, Venice, Vienna, Berlin, and even Sicily. The varied datelines gave the reader the sense that the *Trib* was truly covering the Continent. Paris was the hub and all the major capitals were the spokes of the wheel.

One of the paper's more famous circulation promotions was to outfit pretty young women in yellow sweaters with the words "Herald Tribune" printed on them. The young women would start hawking the paper around midnight to all the cafés. I am not too sure how many papers were sold, but they attracted a lot of attention, and even inspired a Jean-Luc Godard film titled *Breathless* with Jean Seberg.

Seberg played an innocent *Trib* girl who fell in love with a French cad, who stole automobiles and killed a cop. After helping her lover steal a few cars, she turned him in to the police. She wore the *Trib* colors throughout the film.

When the picture first came out, I took issue with the bad image Seberg gave the paper. I protested that we would never hire anyone to sell our papers who was mixed up with a French gangster.

To prove my point, I published an application that the salesgirls had to fill out. It began:

"Have you ever stolen a car?"

If they said no, I then asked, "Are you now living with anyone who ever killed a policeman?" If their reply was negative, they automatically got a job.

Selling *Herald Tribune*s after midnight was a dangerous business, and almost every one of the saleswomen was propositioned by somebody.

I witnessed a scene at Alexander's late one evening. A tall, statuesque Norwegian girl was going from table to table, when a German tourist pinched her bottom. She picked up a bottle of red wine from his table and poured it slowly over his head until it was empty. The other tables cheered, and as a token of our admiration, our table bought every paper she had.

The *Tribune* never made a great deal of money. The various currencies fluctuated so much that one day we'd make a killing on the paper in Spain and the next day lose money on a devaluation in Portugal. The difference between black and red for the paper in the fifties was that the Marshall Plan bought several thousand subscriptions to send out to people of influence in Europe. This was a cheap way to get America's story across, and the *Trib* had credibility that the U.S. government did not.

Everyone was happy with the arrangement, until the *New York Times* started an edition in Europe to compete with us. It was as dull as you could get, but the *Times*' owners demanded half the Marshall Plan subscriptions. The USIA had to give them their share, but all hell broke loose with the readers. Everyone from the British Parliament to the French foreign office was furious that their *Trib* subscription had been taken away and had been substituted for by the *Times,* which was nothing more than a replate of the New York paper.

I lived through half a dozen publishers sent over from New York to "improve" the European edition. It took them six months to realize it was an impossible publication to change, and that no matter what they fiddled with, it had a life and personality of its own.

I remember once returning from a farewell lunch for editor Bill Weeks, who'd been recalled to the United States. I walked with Phil Weld, who had just arrived to take over and was hell-bent on changing everything. I said cheerfully to him, "Don't worry, Phil, in twelve months we'll give a farewell luncheon for you."

The rue de Berri was a busy street at eleven-thirty to midnight, when Americans came to the building to get their paper fresh off the presses. Many of the customers played the stock market. Others were readers who had to have a taste of home. We were the lifeboat, the anchor, the savior of so many who felt better just by reading an English-speaking paper to make sure everything was all right.

One evening I was making the rounds of the night clubs. Bare breasts were a big thing in France for Americans, who never got to see any in the United States. I got bored with them early in my career and longed to see showgirls with clothes on. Many clubs had nude mannequins who just sulked around the floor to some lousy music. The dancers were not topless and put on a better show.

By today's standard, there wasn't too much erotic stuff going on in the clubs, but it was still more than you could get at home. I found very sophisticated Americans who were dying to see a pride of bosoms marching down the Lido runway. The hardest part of my job was to review the club shows and make them sound worth seeing. The only exceptions were the Moulin Rouge, the Lido, and the Crazy Horse Saloon.

There were many minefields for me on the rue de Berri. Just after I turned off the Champs-Elysées, I ran into a restaurant called the Jour et Nuit, which stayed open all night. In front of the Jour, on the sidewalk, were nine or ten prostitutes selling their services. In order to get to the paper, I had to fight my way through the ladies. They were strong on marketing, and always tried to trip me as I went by.

When I told them that I wasn't interested in what they were selling, they would yell at me. "If you do it with your hand, you'll save a lot of money."

One evening there was a transportation strike, and I was at the Hôtel George-V trying to figure out a way of getting to the Tour d'Argent, seven miles away.

There were no taxis, but a prostitute who drove a smashing red Fiat convertible came by and asked me if I wanted some action.

I said, "Not at the moment, but I'll make a deal with you. If you take me to the Tour d'Argent, I'll pay you the same as if you committed sexual favors on my person."

She had a sense of humor, and agreed — and we went whizzing through Paris, laughing at the whole idea.

When we got there, I gave her the equivalent of $30 (sex for Americans was very reasonable in those days). She put the money in her brassiere, kissed me on the cheek, and said, "This is better than working."

Here's my final hooker story. A Paris-based manager for an American movie company was contacted by his studio in Hollywood and told that a very important TV station owner was coming to Paris alone. The manager was to give the man anything he wanted, within reason, and bill the studio.

The TV man showed up, and said his only request was to have a female companion for dinner. The agent rang up a call girl on the office entertainment list and told her to go to dinner with the man, but that whatever happened she was not to ask for money. He was to compensate her in the morning, and since he was tying up her entire evening, he would pay three times what she received for one session.

The next morning, the girl came in and the manager counted out the equivalent of $200. The following morning, he gave the lady another $200. After five mornings of this, the agent was going over budget. So he called up the Hollywood TV visitor and said, "How are you doing with the girl I introduced you to?"

"Just great," he said. "I think I'm going to get lucky tonight."

When I first started writing my *Trib* pieces, I mistakenly thought that tourists were far more interested in night life than in restaurants, so I devoted the column to reviewing such places as the Bal Tabarin, the Lido, and the Folies-Bergère.

The best of the night club columns dealt with the Bal Tabarin. The press agent called and told me they were initiating "Amateur Strip Tease" every Thursday night. Shop girls, models, stewardesses, and school teachers were to compete for the French franc equivalent of $50 by taking off their clothes in front of the audience.

On opening night, three or four amateurs came out, and finally a very cute nurse started to take off her clothes. The band played a medley of strip songs, and the nurse dropped one shoe, then the other, and started to roll her stocking down. In the middle of doing this, she burst into tears and ran offstage, while everyone applauded. (The amateur stripper with the most applause won.)

At the end of the show, just before the winner was announced, the same nurse came back on the stage, and with a look of determination, started tearing off all her clothes. The crowd went crazy and of course the nurse won the $50.

I wrote about this, and some friends asked me to take them the following week, which I did. We sat back relaxed — and then I could not believe my eyes. The same nurse from the previous week was on stage, doing her number and bursting into tears and running off-stage. It was the first striptease show I saw that was fixed. If I'd wanted a scoop, I would have revealed the scam. But the audience seemed to be having such a good time, I said, "The heck with it. It's a much better evening for the readers if no one knows the truth."

The most expensive of the Paris night clubs were Les Grands Seigneurs and Monseigneur and Shéhérazade. They featured violinists from Russia and Hungary. Fifteen or twenty of them would surround your table and play romantic songs, while the leader and the first violinist poured glasses from your bottle and passed them around to members of the orchestra. The customer would wind up paying $200 to $4,300 for the evening. A friend of mine complained about his bill, and said that in the future he would keep the corks of his bottles in his pocket after he had consumed the wine. The management agreed. The next time he came in, he started drinking, and while he consumed one bottle the management kept sneaking corks into his pockets, and once again he got burned with an enormous check.

The best show was the Lido. I had the honor of taking Elvis Presley there. He was wearing his U.S. Army uniform and was on leave from Germany. I had interviewed him for the paper and then invited him out on the town.

After the performance, I took him backstage to the dressing room of the Bluebell girls, who went nuts. They were all over him, vying to have the singer take them back to the hotel, though none of them got lucky. I was hoping that his rejects might ask me to take them home, but whatever attraction he held for women, I didn't. In those days, Elvis was a shy, modest man and the army treated him with kid gloves.

I have very rarely been able to get a rise out of my children concerning the people I met in Europe, but a hush falls over the room when I talk about my evening with Elvis.

One of my toughest experiences as a tour guide for VIPs took place one night with Lew Wasserman and his wife, Edie. Wasserman was head of MCA, then a talent agency, before it became a media conglomerate.

I said, "I will take you to the Crazy Horse Saloon, the greatest striptease joint in the free world."

We arrived to find the crowds all jamming up the sidewalk waiting to get in. I was desperate — I jumped the line and found the owner and told him that my job was at stake if I didn't get a table.

He gave me one practically on the stage. The Wassermans fought their way through the mob, while the rest of the room booed us. We sat down, and two French comedians came onstage and started telling French jokes.

Wasserman said, "Let's get out of here."

"Wait," I begged. "The striptease comes next. It's fantastic."

Lew and Edie got up and wrestled their way out of the room, while the crowd booed again.

"Well, hot shot," Lew said, "where to now?"

"Do you like French jazz? I'll take you

to the Rose Rouge." It took us fifteen minutes to arrive at the Left Bank cave. We went downstairs, and as we looked up at the stage, we saw the same two comedians we had just left at the Crazy Horse Saloon, telling the same jokes. Obviously, they were doubling and doing it by motorcycle.

Lew just turned around and walked out.

On the street, he turned to me and said, "Thanks for the lovely evening. Next time, Edie and I will take the 'Paris by Night' American Express tour."

Before I go any further, I will warn the reader that while I have already done some name-dropping in this book, there will be a great deal more. I am not copping a plea. The names belong to people with whom I hung out and ate lunches and dinners and wrote about in Paris. Some were not famous at the time, but became famous afterwards. I was an American columnist based in Paris, writing a people-oriented column for an English-language newspaper. Therefore, my professional and social life, and to some extent my family life, were all taken up with the celebrities of the times.

The so-called International Set consisted not only of the beautiful and empty-headed people but also of the most powerful men and women in the world. They could buy and sell heads of countries, and usually did. They sold oil and gold and marks and yen and boatloads of guns and ammunition, and they laundered money and acquired and disposed of mistresses to their heart's content.

They moved their fortunes and businesses around to avoid taxes, and they bought diplomats by the barrel. As far as they were concerned, the laws did not apply to them, and they had on their payrolls dozens of lawyers and judges and ex-prime ministers to keep them out of jail.

Some were self-made — others were titled, who often had little money but did a wonderful job of pretending they did.

I made no judgments on their morals or ethics, preferring instead to concentrate on their extravagances and ostentatious displays of wealth.

Like so many Americans who lived abroad, I accepted whatever people were doing with a certain tolerance, which might have disturbed me had these same people been fleecing the United States.

One of my heroes was Thornton Wilder. One day in the fifties, we were in St. Moritz in a fancy ski club. He tried to explain to me what the members of the International Set were all about.

"Archie," he said (he was the only person who ever called me Archie), "what you see all around you is the same proportion of hopeless self-destructive waste as opposed to amiable contacts and loveable, rewarding human beings. I have never believed that poverty totally destroys nor that wealth totally corrupts.

"But, Archie, we must differentiate between those who have wealth and those who live for pleasure. Unhappily, those who live for pleasure are always looking over their shoulders, in the hopes of finding the pleasure somewhere else.

"The mystic feeling concerning birth and privilege is disappearing. In years gone by, nobody questioned that the rich were God's children.

"But now they have to be reassured

as to who they really are by writers like yourself." Then he put his hand on my shoulder and said, "Archie, the rich need you more than you need them."

What contributed to the feeling that my life was slightly unbelievable was that most of the celebrities who visited Paris often appeared uncomfortable in such unfamiliar surroundings — and I was one of the few people with whom they could feel any kinship. I was an American, I spoke their language, and I wasn't after gossip or scandal.

Someone would come to Paris — Lucille Ball, say — and she would send Milton Berle, who would send Mike Todd and Joan Blondell, etc. The visitors weren't just show-business personalities, but CEOs of America's largest corporations, senators and congressmen, governors, novelists, professional tennis players. All of us became very cozy, and I dropped their names and they dropped mine.

How did I feel about this? I felt like I was riding a horse in a steeplechase. I could hardly catch my breath after finishing a conversation with J. Paul Getty before starting a new one with Truman Capote.

One of my favorite couples in the International Set was the Duke and Duchess of Windsor. The duchess was very bright and tough, and, I thought, very attractive. I liked her because she said what was on her mind. She also invited me to dinner.

The duke, on the other hand, was a dimwit who appeared not to know about anything that was going on and never said one word that was memorable. I recall how after dinner, when we would all be gathered in his living room for coffee and cognac, he would burst into German songs. I sat there smiling, but the thought ran through my head, "The horse's ass still loves Germany."

The second thought was that the English should build a statue to Wallis Simpson on Trafalgar Square for saving the Commonwealth from having the duke as their king.

I really loved mingling with the very rich. One evening, I was sitting at a table in the bar at St. Mortiz with Gianni Agnelli, the Fiat CEO; Fritz Opel of the automobile Opels; Stavros Niarchos, the shipping magnate; and Count Theo Rossi of Martini & Rossi vermouth.

It was two o'clock in the morning, and everyone else in the bar had a date. Our table was womanless. I said, "I can't believe it. Here we are, with an estimated four billion dollars between us, and not one person at this table is going to get laid tonight."

What helped to make my job such a lark was that most of the people I took out believed I really knew something about food and wine. My background as a foster child, an enlisted man in the Marines, and a student at USC had not exactly prepared me for this role of *bon vivant* in Paris, but I rose to the task.

When I studied a menu, I always followed the same ritual. "Are the asparagus fresh?" I would ask the captain, knowing damn well he would say, "Yes." Then I would ask, "Would you recommend them hot or cold?"

I had everyone's attention. Then I might say, "When were the quail shot?" or sternly, "When you cook the lamb, make sure it's very pink. Don't bring it to me red or brown, just p-i-n-k."

Even Jim Beard, the food writer and chef, was impressed. I usually left the wine selection to the sommelier by saying, "Jean, could you perhaps dig up something in that filthy cellar of yours that can do justice to this *steak au poivre?*"

My guests were bursting to applaud. Little did they know that my entire childhood, except for my vegetarian period with the Seventh-Day Adventists, had been spent eating leftover meatloaf in Queens, New York.

I loved to discuss French wine. My past experience with alcohol was summed up by the moonshine I'd drunk in the Marines in the Central Pacific, the beer I'd tasted at USC off-campus bars, and the slivovitz rotgut I'd consumed at the Hôtel des États-Unis. So I did what any self-respecting wine buff did. I faked it.

In the beginning, I knew little about wine, so I memorized the names of the most prominent ones, which I mentioned at will. It worked so well that I was made a member of the Confrérie des Chevaliers du Tastevin, an organization whose sole purpose was to promote burgundies.

My installation was held at a dinner in Dijon at the stately Château of Clos Vougeot. I was very nervous, because I was afraid they would discover that I was a fraud. I didn't eat all day. Instead, I read books about wine and practiced phrases such as "This is exactly the bouquet I have been searching for all my life," and "I shall never forget the La Tâche my grandfather served Marshall Foch on his seventy-fifth birthday."

The chateau courtyard was lit with torches. After Puligny-Montrachet aperitifs, we were ushered into the grand hall for dinner. Across from me was an officer of the Order of the Chevaliers. He was three times my age and a severe grump. He did not believe Americans belonged there.

I was starving, and the first course was *quenelles de brochet,* with lobster sauce. The old man was served first, and said, "This is terrible. Not fit for a pig." He looked at me. "Don't eat it."

"Don't eat it?" I said.

The waiter came by, and I shook my head. My mouth watered and I fought back the rumbling in my stomach. Others at the table did not seem to have any problem with the *quenelles.*

The next course was *duck à l'orange* served with souffléd potatoes and tender green peas. Once again, the martinet tasted first, threw his knife and fork down, and declared, "This is not *duck à l'orange,* it is roasted crow."

I didn't care what it was. I wanted to tear it apart with my bare hands.

Once again, he said sternly, "Don't eat it."

"What about the souffléd potatoes?" I asked.

"They're cold, don't eat them."

The entire meal continued in the same vein. I kept drinking wine, though I had no food to go with it. Every time someone raised a glass to toast my induction, I raised mine to my lips. It didn't take long to get swacked on the burgundy. Even the dessert was not to my tablemate's liking, so I passed on that, too.

By the time the final ceremonies began, I was giddy. I went up to get my wine taster's cup, and I think I said, "I'd rather starve to death than eat *quenelles de brochet* that weren't cooked to my taste." The audience seemed to like this, and applauded me with enthusiasm.

I got back to the hotel in Dijon at eleven and called down to the kitchen for something to eat.

"It's closed," said the concierge.

When I wrote about my experience, the Chevalier people were very upset, and there was talk about stripping me of my winetaster's cup. But I did make one contribution to Burgundy — I heard the Chevaliers fired the caterer.

Bordeaux winemakers have little use for Burgundy vintners, and vice versa. One of my friends was Alexis Lichine, who started out his professional life as a dealer of French wines in the U.S., wrote many wonderful books about wine, and was a romantic figure with all sorts of ladies. Eventually, he bought a vineyard of his own — the Château Prieuré-Lichine and Lascombes, where he bottled several respectable wines.

I was his guest, and Alexis, who knew all the great growers in Bordeaux, took me on a tour of their chateaux and caves.

Lichine gave me a short course in the economics of wine. "When it's a poor year for wine, caused by severe weather, the price goes up, because there is a shortage of drinkable vintage. When it's a great weather year, and there is an abundance of grapes and all the elements are in our favor, the price also goes up."

"Why is that?"

"Because everybody fights to buy a good year."

Lichine briefed me on wine-tasting in his own cellars. "Always swish the wine around in your mouth clockwise for Bordeaux, counter-clockwise for Burgundy. Never swallow it; spit it out."

We went to the Château Margaux and the Château Latour, and I spat. Lichine was pleased with his pupil. Our last stop was Château Mouton-Rothschild, owned by Philippe de Rothschild. Mr. Rothschild, a charming host, showed us through his caves and then invited us to an elegantly furnished glass salon overlooking all his vineyards. One of the many priceless items in the room was an eighteenth-century rug. A servant came by and handed me a glass of champagne. I swished it around in my mouth. Lichine looked at me in horror, and screamed, "NO!"

It was too late. I spat it on the carpet.

Years later, my article about spitting on his rug appeared in the French *Reader's Digest.* Rothschild was so impressed he had a case of Mouton Rothschild 1959 delivered to my house in Washington. I put it in the cellar. No one who came to my home was worthy of a bottle.

At the time, the Vietnam war was raging in earnest, and my children and their friends cared little for anything. One day, I was up in the attic and I saw in the corner a pile of empty wine bottles. In disbelief, I realized they had once contained my Rothschild wine. I let out a blood-curdling scream, went downstairs, and confronted my daughter. "Why did you take my French wine from the cellar?" I demanded.

She said, "We couldn't find any Blue Nun."

When I finally cut back on night clubs, I added more restaurants to my column and the reaction was immediate. Everyone picked up on a tip in my column. I literally made French establishments by plugging them. What confused many proprietors was that although they read or had someone read the writeup to them, they had no idea who I was and couldn't understand why I hadn't introduced myself so they could slip me some smoked salmon.

To keep me honest, the *Tribune* insisted that I pay for my meals and gave me an expense account. Some of the French gourmands who wrote about food were on the take.

Paris has thousands of restaurants, and it was impossible to cover them all. What saved me was that tourists became my touts and sent in tips about places they had eaten in and liked. Most of them were excellent, and I relied on my mail to lead me to new gastronomic heavens.

One of my favorite discoveries during those incredible years was a rundown bistro in the Bastille area called Chez l'Ami Louis. A reader recommended it to me, and even with my lack of training in good food, I knew I had hit upon one of the most wondrous restaurants in Europe. All the food came from the region of Landes. The *foie gras* made French gastronomes shiver with excitement. The frogs' legs doused in garlic will always remain on its own page in my memory book. To this day, I have never eaten *petit pois* comparable to those served with the roasted chicken at Chez l'Ami Louis.

I wrote an ecstatic article on the restaurant, which sent Americans there in large numbers, much to the disgust of those who'd known about it before-hand. The regular patrons hated me for revealing their secret.

A few days before the article appeared, I received a call from Darryl Zanuck. "Give me the name of a restaurant Americans haven't heard of."

I told him, "Chez l'Ami Louis."

The next Sunday evening, I showed up, and at every table was a movie star from Twentieth Century-Fox.

"What are you doing here?" Danny Kaye asked me.

"I discovered it," I said defensively.

"Bullshit," he said. "Darryl Zanuck found this place, and he made us swear that we would never tell anyone else."

Sometimes, discovering a restaurant did not guarantee good treatment for me. I wrote about a wonderful bistro on the Seine called l'Ourse Martin. That night, friends suggested we go there. I called, and the woman said brusquely, "No tables."

"But," I protested, "I was the man in the *Herald Tribune* who wrote about your restaurant this morning."

"I know," she said. "That's why I have no tables," and she hung up.

By this time I wasn't just reviewing

restaurants, I had become part of the action. For instance, I took a course at the Cordon Bleu, the famed cooking school, where I had an entire seminar on how to break an egg.

I also talked Maxim's into letting me be a waiter for a night. It was an eye-opening experience. I discovered that the patrons never paid attention to the waiter and continued their conversations as if nobody was there. These included business secrets, as well as matters of the heart: "I intend to tell my wife about us tonight, chérie." I also observed that men wooing women were more likely to splurge on expensive wine than those who were with their wives.

One of the reasons I was so sure nobody paid attention to a waiter was that there were several people in the restaurant that I knew. None of them even recognized me.

Another three-star restaurant in Paris was the Tour d'Argent, France's highest-priced restaurant, which overlooked the Cathedral of Notre Dame. It was run by a handsome rake who earned his three stars not only with food but with women. He became one of my idols, not just because he knew so much about haute cuisine but because he was so skilled in charming his female diners. His bedroom was one floor down from his restaurant. The women who came to the Tour without a male companion (usually at lunch) seemed happy to visit both floors. Under the circumstances, that in itself was not remarkable. What I found remarkable was that the owner always waited until the women paid their checks before he made his move.

I once asked him about that, and he said, "It wouldn't be the same if I thought they were doing it for a free pressed duck."

One of the beauties of France is that the bistro food is as good as the Michelin-starred restaurants. Many are mom-and-pop, mom-and-son, pop-and-daughter, and entire-family res-taurants.

Everything in France tastes better. Once I was asked on a TV show about the greatest meal I had ever had in Paris, and I said that it had been a slice of duck pâté on a buttered *baguette* with sour pickles and a glass of pilsner beer.

It is impossible to spend time in

France without becoming attached to the French loaf of bread. Bread is to the French what the umbrella is to the British. It is carried at all times, rain or shine, and has many functions. You can hail a taxi with a loaf of bread, use it as a weapon if you are attacked, signal a friend across the street, or present arms when the president of France goes by.

The *ficelle* is the thinnest, and is perfect for pointing out things to a friend or sticking out to signal you are about to make a left turn.

The *baguette* is the most popular — thicker, with more body, and used as you would a rifle, or, if you have had a skiing accident, a cane.

A French bread scene I'll always remember is the time I watched a man on a motor scooter with a *baguette* sticking out of his knapsack. As he stopped at a red light, the man behind him on another scooter leaned forward and began to break off and eat his loaf of bread.

You could go north, south, east, or west in Paris and rarely get a bad meal. One night, I was challenged by baked-bean heir Jack Heinz and his friend Les

Gruber, the owner of the London Chop House in Detroit, to provide them with a night they would never forget.

"Give us a gastronomic experience like no American has ever had in Paris," Jack challenged me.

I thought about it, and said, "Hire a car. This is going to take some doing."

First, I took them to Rech, near the Arc de Triomphe, a fish restaurant noted for its Belon oysters. Then on to the Tour d'Argent for a black carrot soup. This was followed by filet of sole at the Mediterranée. After that, we went to Taillevent for *noisettes d'agneau,* and on to l'Escargot for asparagus with béarnaise sauce, and then we drove to Androuët, the incredible cheese restaurant near the Gare St-Lazare. We wound up with *crêpes suzettes* at Maxim's, and finally coffee and brandy at Fouquet's. Because I was the food critic of the *Herald Tribune* and known to these restaurants, we were permitted to have only one course at these establishments without the waiters pouring soup down our necks.

In a few years, I had achieved a certain fame as a food critic. When serious food writers such as Craig Claiborne came to town, I was their escort. The lady who created Pepperidge Farms bread requested that I take her to French bakeries, and the man who owned the Sara Lee company asked me to help him find the perfect French cheesecake, which does not exist in France.

But I blew my chance of receiving the French Legion of Honor when I proclaimed a restaurant in Brussels as the greatest in Europe. It was called L'Épaule de Mouton, and was located in a seventeenth-century building on a tiny street behind the Grand Palais. I stuck my neck out on this, because L'Épaule had no more than seven tables and could only seat twenty-eight people. The dinner was orchestrated by Monsieur Chanteraine and his uncle, known as Uncle René. Instead of serving dishes that already existed in the culinary world, the two men had created their own — seventy-six in number. All the dishes were cooked in front of the patrons in the small room.

The secret of the food rested with the two men, and could not be duplicated by anyone. The first night I was there, I had lobster Leopold II, made with cream sauce, flambéed with Pernod, and curry, truffles, and mushrooms, served on a crown of white rice. For dessert, Uncle René created a new flavor crêpe with calvados. All this came with one of the restaurant's best bottles of wine.

The column caused more of a stir than I had anticipated. Every great restaurant, from Sweden to Italy, could not believe that I had the audacity to give the blue ribbon to Belgium. But readers of the *Trib* flocked there, some waiting months to get in. Monsieur Chanteraine was so impressed that he named a dish after me — Filet de sole à la Buchwald.

When my Left Bank friends read this, they were furious.

"Where do you come off naming the best restaurant in Europe?" they would ask.

I replied, "If God didn't want me to do it, he would not have given me my extremely sensitive palate."

In the spring of 1994, I went back to L'Épaule de Mouton, but it was no more. Uncle René had gone to that great kitchen in the sky, the owner had retired, and Filet de sole à la Buchwald was nowhere to be found. It was nothing more than a gastronomic memory, and in time will be forgotten even in Belgian folklore.

Some other friends of mine were planning a very unique way of seeing France. Bill Lewis, the chairman of the Kenyon and Eckhart advertising agency, and his wife decided that they wanted to visit every Michelin three-star restaurant in the country. At that time, there were eight in France, and it took five weeks to get around to them.

I was so proud of the Lewises that I decided on their return to Paris to drape their necks with the "Order of the Three-Star Liver" in a ceremony at the Lasserre Restaurant. But I needed a medal, so I went to a store next to Harry's New York Bar on the rue Daunou.

I studied the contents of the glass cases and finally chose a green ribbon with a bronze medal attached. The medal depicted a man harvesting wheat. It was the Medaille de Mérite Agricole.

I told the clerk that I would take it.

He said indignantly, "Monsieur, did you earn this medal?"

"No," I replied. "It's a joke."

"A joke! Farmers have died for this medal. They have given their blood, their hearts, and the sweat of their bodies to earn it — and you call it a joke."

I was embarrassed, and said, "You're right, and I apologize for my insensitivity. Forget it."

I started to walk out of the store, when he yelled, "I have a Victoria Cross if you would like it."

I sometimes tried spicing up my food column with controversies. One concerned the differences between the French and British when it came to dining. I pointed out that the French serve cheese before the dessert, while the British serve cheese after. I maintained that this was because the French drive on the right side of the road and the British on the left. I said that it probably didn't matter, unless the British tourist suddenly found himself eating his cheese first.

This produced a hailstorm of mail, including one irate letter from London, which said, "It's nobody's damn business when we eat our cheese. By serving the cheese last, we, as usual, are right and the French are wrong."

There was more confusion when I heard from a diplomat in Nigeria who said that where he was stationed people ate the meat course after the dessert, and drove in the middle of the road.

I kept up the controversy for weeks and involved the British ambassador in France, who tried to solve the dilemma by suggesting that everyone eat savories.

One of my more enjoyable battles in the column took place in March 1958, when someone at the American army base in Verdun sent me a memo from headquarters warning the soldiers not to eat French food that could possibly be contaminated. The doctors on the base claimed that French food that was not properly treated could be full of bacteria, and if eaten by G.I.s might result in terrible consequences.

I picked up the ball, and made fun of the army for taking such a downbeat view of French food and restaurants. I told the soldiers to ignore their medical advisors. The American brass were furious, because they had become the laughing stock of Europe. Letters were dispatched to the *Herald Tribune.* The colonel who wrote the orders said that his first duty was to keep soldiers from getting sick on French food.

I was the heavy, and the target of the army's wrath. The controversy came to a crashing halt when I came down with hepatitis and had to seek treatment at the American Hospital. From the army's point of view, the timing could not have been better, and their medical experts used my illness to prove how dangerous French food could be.

But I think that the biggest column battle involving French restaurants did not concern the food, but the custom of allowing dogs in the restaurants.

It seems that almost everyone in France takes their dogs to eating establishments, and also insists on feeding them from their own plates. I made the mistake of suggesting that dogs had no place in restaurants and were a health hazard to other patrons. Nothing, not even questioning the virtue of Joan of Arc, caused such a stir. The mail poured into the *Trib*'s office from all parts of the country.

The thrust of the letters was, how dare an American tell the French where their dogs could eat. People claimed that most French pets were far better behaved than American tourists, and also knew more about French food.

One angry reader said that he would no more dine out without his dog than he would without his wife.

If there was any particular theme to my columns, it was that nothing was to be taken seriously. One of my running features concerned the "International Food Patrol" in Vienna. The pieces covered a period in the early fifties when the city was occupied by the Russians, the British, the French, and the Americans. If you saw the movie *The Third Man*, you'll be familiar with the period. The four powers patrolled the city together and it was a tense time for everyone. The city was full of spies with unlimited expense accounts, and everything was for sale.

One evening five of us — Alex Kendrick of CBS, Si Bourgin of *Time* magazine, Franz Spelman of the State Department, Joe Israel of NBC, and I — decided to organize the International Food Patrol, which would deal with food intelligence in the occupied parts of the city.

Kendrick declared, "We cannot fight the Russians unless we know how much paprika they are putting in their Hungarian goulash. It is also our job to find out if the French are selling wiener schnitzel under the table to the British in exchange for layers of sacher torte."

Bourgin agreed. "We will form an International Food Patrol, and on the pretense of doing a story on Polish exiles we will smuggle out Yugoslavian potato pancakes in our typewriter cases."

This was a typical report to me from Al Kendrick concerning Bourgin:

"Dear Art:

"Right after you left Vienna, our garlic expert, Si Bourgin, met a girl. He told us that she was a wonderful person and liked all the things that he liked. As you know, Si is the romantic of the patrol, unlike Spelman, who is serious, and Israel, who is cynical, and you, who are fun-loving.

"Last week, Si and his girl and I went to a Viennese restaurant which had changed its name from Meissel and Schaden to the Capri, for security reasons. In the course of the meal, Bourgin's girl pushed away a plate of garlic, saying that she never touched the stuff, and Bourgin almost had a heart attack. How, I asked, could he possibly be in love with someone who didn't like garlic?

"Si tried to persuade her to try it. He told her that if she didn't like the taste, he would be happy to inject it into her upper thigh. But she adamantly refused. So I was forced to step in. I told Bourgin that I would have to report him to you as associating with an anti-garlic mole. He begged me not to do it, and I was about to reconsider, when his girlfriend started pouring sugar on her lettuce.

"It turns out that Viennese like to put sugar on their salad. The French have known this for years, but have refused to admit it publicly, because if they acknowledged it, everyone would realize that they had broken the Austrian code.

"So there she was eating her sweetened salad but refusing to touch the garlic. I told Bourgin the only out was for him to eat her garlic portion, as well as his own, thus sacrificing a chance for him to make it with her that night — and possibly many more.

"Bourgin went through with it, and he is now in the Krankenhaus in a garlic coma. The doctor gave him sips of a

Bulgarian wine called Plodiv, but he keeps crying out for 'Mitzi.'

"Mitzi was a pig that we ate last week at the Balkan Grill. We didn't know that she meant so much to him. With Bourgin in the hospital, I will cover the American zone. By the way, I found a restaurant in the British zone that had the following sign in its window: 'The Best Food in Town Is at This Place, But We Also Must Inform You That Our Chef Is Extremely Dirty.'

"Respectfully yours, Patrolman Kendrick."

One day in 1953, I thought it would be fun to explain the meaning of the Thanksgiving Day feast to the French. I planned to use fractured French for the purpose. I seem to remember that almost everyone in the city room contributed something to it, so I can't claim sole authorship.

I print it in its entirety.

One of the most important holidays is Thanksgiving Day, known in France as "le Jour de Merci Donnant."

"Le Jour de Merci Donnant" was first started by a group of pilgrims (Pèlerins) who fled from l'Angleterre before the McCarran Act to found a colony in the New World (*le Nouveau Monde*) where they could shoot Indians (*les Peaux-Rouges*) and eat turkey (*dinde*) to their hearts' content.

They landed at a place called Plymouth (now a famous *voiture Américaine*) in a wooden sailing ship named the *Mayflower*, or *Fleur de Mai*, in 1620. But while the *Pèlerins* were killing the *dindes*, the *Peaux-Rouges* were killing the *Pèlerins*, and there were several hard winters ahead for both of them. The only way the *Peaux-Rouges* helped the *Pèlerins* was when they taught them how to grow corn (*maïs*). The reason they did this was because they liked corn with their *Pèlerins*.

In 1623 after another harsh year, the *Pèlerins*' crops were so good that they decided to have a celebration and give thanks because more *maïs* was raised by the *Pèlerins* than *Pèlerins* were killed by the *Peaux-Rouges*.

Every year on "le Jour de Merci Donnant," parents tell their children an amusing story about the first celebration. It concerns a brave *capitaine* named Miles Standish (known in

France as *Kilomètres Deboutish)* and a shy young lieutenant named Jean Alden. Both of them were in love with a flower of Plymouth called Priscilla Mullens (no translation). The *vieux capitaine* said to the *jeune lieutenant:*

"Go to the damsel Priscilla *(Allez très vite chez Priscilla),* the loveliest maiden of Plymouth *(la plus jolie demoiselle de Plymouth).* Say that a blunt old captain, a man not of words but of action *(un vieux Fanfan la Tulipe),* offers his hand and his heart — the hand and heart of a soldier. Not in these words, you understand, but this, in short, is my meaning.

"I am a maker of war *(Je suis un fabricant de la guerre)* and not a maker of phrases. You, bred as a scholar *(Vous, qui êtes pain comme un étudiant),* can say it in elegant language, such as you read in your books of the pleadings and wooings of lovers, such as you think best suited to win the heart of the maiden."

Although Jean was fit to be tied *(convenable à être emballé),* friendship prevailed over love and he went to his duty. But instead of using elegant language, he blurted out his mission. Priscilla was muted with amazement and sorrow *(rendue muette par l'étonnement et la tristesse).*

At length she exclaimed, breaking the ominous silence, "If the great captain of Plymouth is so very eager to wed me, why does he not come himself and take the trouble to woo me?" *(Où est-il, le vieux Kilomètres? Pourquoi ne vient-il pas auprès de moi pour tenter sa chance?)*

Jean said that *Kilomètres Deboutish* was very busy and didn't have time for such things. He staggered on, telling her what a wonderful husband *Kilomètres* would make. Finally, Priscilla arched her eyebrows and said in a tremulous voice, "Why don't you speak for yourself, Jean?" *(Chacun à son gout.)*

And so, on the fourth Thursday in November, American families sit down at a large table brimming with tasty dishes, and for the only time during the year eat better than the French do.

No one can deny that "le Jour de Merci Donnant" is a *grand fête* and no matter how well-fed American families are, they never forget to give thanks to *Kilomètres Deboutish,* who made this great day possible.

The first year it was received so well that I decided to print it again, and again and again. We're talking forty-three years! Some people love it, some hate it, but editors have been reluctant to refuse to print it, because I told them that if they didn't run it, they would have forty years of bad Thanksgiving Day dinners.

While no one has ever voiced any objection to this column, there was one that the *Trib* absolutely refused to run. Like most American institutions in the early fifties, the *Herald Tribune* was deathly afraid of Senator Joseph McCarthy. Actually, they were afraid of the *Trib* readers who were afraid of McCarthy. I've been waiting all these years to print it.

I wrote:

"If you want to learn the real truth about Senator McCarthy, the place to go is Ireland. There have been McCarthies and rumors of McCarthies since 123 A.D., when Eoghan the Splendid, born of the race of Heber, emerged from the gloom and slime of the most mythical period in Irish history.

"But, as in every family, there is one bad seed. It was planted in 1203 when Donal Mor Ma Curra took it into his head to hold a witchhunt and slay 160 diplomats who he maintained were traitors to the crown.

"There is worse to come. Finn McCarthy was slain by his own brothers, and they in turn were killed by their own cousins, and so on ad infinitum. They were an ugly lot. Derman surrendered his son as hostage to the English king and Lough Din was sold to the enemy in exchange for a herd of cows on the Normandy coast.

"Every one of these McCarthies committed unspeakable acts.

"During the potato famine, the entire bad strain wound up in America, and no one knows where they are now."

There was only one other column, as I recall, that never made it into the paper and it concerned my confession in 1949 that I had marched in an East Berlin parade. I was caught up in the crowd, I explained, and had no choice but to scream epithets against Americans and imperialism as I passed by the Communist Party reviewing stand. I thought it had a nice Charlie Chaplin quality to it, but New York wasn't buying it.

George Cornish, the managing editor, wrote, "In the tense international situation, a large number of people would have almost surely misunderstood your marching in a Communist parade in East Berlin. Naturally, I completely understood your position, and I think that more than a majority of our readers would have done so. Yet there would have been the very real chance that some thousands of our readers would not have done so. It hardly seemed worthwhile to invite trouble."

I would be remiss in this chapter about my days on the *Trib* not to mention how parsimonious the *Herald Tribune* really was, both in New York and Paris. One of my prize collections is a large envelope stuffed with letters from a number of *Trib* editors and business managers such as Bill Weeks, Sylvan Barnett, Bernice Cutler, Andre Bing, Phil Welch, and others over the last forty-five years, explaining why they couldn't pay me a decent salary. We're talking such sums as $15 and $20 a week. They would tell us that the financial condition of the New York paper prevented them from rewarding anyone with a raise for his or her work.

The letters took on a pattern, and pretty soon I knew what was in them before opening the envelope. The first two paragraphs from the editor lauded my column and told me of the great reaction it was getting in the U.S.

The third paragraph almost always began with "Unfortunately," and went on to describe the precarious financial state of the paper and this was not the time to throw dollars around when there was still so much belt-tightening to do.

For as long as I worked on it, the Paris *Herald Tribune* was either suffering from a weak franc, a sick British pound, or a crippled Italian lira, and, as always, the time was not right to pay out any of the cash to the help.

Chapter 4

Ann

In 1950, I had no particular lady friend in Paris and went out with anyone who would have me. It was less difficult to get dates there than it was at USC. Women tourists were desperate to see as much of Paris as they could, and so their standards of a respectable escort became lower and lower as their tour wound down. I know this because some of America's most beautiful daughters, who wouldn't have told me the time under the Biltmore clock, were friendly, warm, and flattering. I spoke with such authority in Franglais when dealing with Parisians that many of the women I took out really believed I understood the language.

One of the women I dated was a fashion writer with the *Philadelphia Bulletin* named Kitty Campbell Mock. She came over twice a year to cover the Paris fashion world, and I first met her at a cocktail party for the designer Jacques Fath. She was petite and very attractive. Like many other women alone in Paris, she found me an eligible escort. We went out to dinner, drank champagne in Russian night clubs, and ate onion soup in the wee hours of the morning at Les Halles — all on the *Philadelphia Bulletin*'s generous expense account. I attended the couture shows with Kitty, and thanks to her I was able to circulate with a better class of people than those I lived with in Montparnasse.

Store department buyers, fashion writers, and dress manufacturers came to Paris twice a year to view the creations of the great French designers — Balmain, Fath, Chanel, Givenchy, Schiaparelli, Balenciaga, and the Great One, Christian Dior. The dresses they bought for five and ten thousand dollars were then shipped home, ripped apart, and adapted and copied for the American consumer. The French designers only made money on the one outfit they sold. That is why the clothes cost so much and that is also why the designers' perfume business became far more lucrative than their clothes.

The fashion audience was made up of free-spending Americans, many of whom were Seventh Avenue dress manufacturers. They were treated royally by the French, particularly when the American dollar played such a large part in Franco-American relations. Fashion news was hot news, because the Americans followed the French designers, and even the length of a skirt could cause all of Seventh Avenue to tremble. The most famous of the nuclear bombs was when Christian Dior lowered his skirts and called it "the new look," sending every fashion buyer and writer into orbit. The move caused world headlines, debate, and confusion. If Dior went long and everyone else stayed short, long-legged women, as we knew them, would never be the same. Alas, Dior's length prevailed, and for several years a lady's knee never saw the sun.

The subject of fashion and the opportunity to spoof it gave me many columns.

When Christian Dior introduced the "Flat Look" and did away with bosoms, this limerick was recited around town:

A man named Christian Dior
Said of bosoms he wanted
  no more.
He did away with lust
By replacing the bust
With a piece of wood from
  the floor.

One evening I was in Kitty's suite at the Plaza-Athénée when a very attractive red-headed Irish-American girl named Ann McGarry, from Warren, Pennsylvania, walked in. She was a friend of Kitty's, and had worked at Neiman Marcus as a fashion coordinator before quitting to come to Paris with $1,000 to learn the couture business. I thought I was polite, but according to her, I was slouched in a chair and didn't bother to get up when she came in. I told her years later that there was a good reason for this. I never expected to see her again, so what was the sense in getting up? Whenever I repeated this remark to any group, she threw bread at me. The three of us had a drink, but no more.

The next time I saw the redhead, she

was eating alone in the Relais Plaza, the fancy grill in the Plaza-Athénée. I stopped by the table and said, "If you keep eating here, your trust fund won't last for more than a week."

She said curtly, "It's none of your business."

I sat down anyway and asked her what she thought of my last column in the *Tribune*.

The third time I saw her was on the Champs-Elysées on a Saturday night about nine o'clock. I was sitting at a sidewalk café and she walked by. I invited her to join me, and I spent the rest of the evening telling her how I had given up a promising career in Hollywood to come to Paris to write a great novel, which would eventually make me famous and a household name in *The New York Times Book Review*.

I told her modestly that I was the food and wine expert of the *Herald Tribune*, and I offered to take her to one of Paris's great restaurants, on the *Trib*'s expense account. She revealed much later in the relationship that she'd thought I was brash, egotistical, and someone who was definitely on the make.

I found her extremely attractive, and

since she wasn't buying any of my routine, I also found her interesting. We stayed in the café until midnight.

Then I took her home to the apartment near the Bastille where she was boarding with a French family. They were miserable snobs and had been recommended by some rich people in Texas who thought they were very proper for Ann to stay with.

One reason I was so bitter was that Ann had to be in at midnight or the concierge would not let her enter the premises. The situation also irritated me because it was a very expensive taxi ride for me, and I made a mental note that if I was going to continue our courtship I would have her meet me at the Métro stop on the Champs-Elysées.

I wanted to see her again because many things about her appealed to me. She was pretty and very bright, and after she decided I would not harm her, she laughed at all my jokes.

That Sunday morning I called her up and said I had been assigned by the French cardinal to make sure every good Catholic girl went to church. I told her the cardinal had made me his messenger because the only people he could trust in Paris were those of the Jewish faith.

She had told me her landlady was out of town for the weekend, so I suggested that after church she stop by the market and buy some food so that she could cook me dinner. I came on so fast she couldn't think of any reason why it was out of the question. It was a very good meal, and we drank a bottle of inexpensive Beaujolais, which I had brought with me. I do remember there were candles on the table. After dinner, I blew out the candles, and in the cold, dark apartment, I made a pass at her, and after some skirmishing, we fell into each other's arms and made love.

The timing for our meeting was perfect. I was lonely and ready to fall in love. I knew this because after meeting Ann, the bread tasted better, the air smelled sweeter, the Seine flowed more gently, and every Parisian looked like a friend. Paris is the best place for kissing in the street and under the bridges and in front of large churches and museums. The French approve of seeing two people in an embrace, as it confirms their own belief that the city is still the capital of love. Ann and I walked through Paris late in the afternoon, late into the night, and early in the morning — stopping every few feet to hug and kiss. Not one person objected, and even the gendarmes nodded their approval.

The game for me was to surprise her. I might grab her in the corner of the Louvre, or kiss her on the steps leading into the Métro. Or better still, rub her back at the Sacré-Coeur overlooking all of Paris. In New York City, this behavior might have been considered inappropriate. In Los Angeles, the only place you could steal a kiss was when you were stalled in traffic on the freeway. In Paris, the citizens positively approved of open displays of affection at any location.

In Warren, Pennsylvania, and even Dallas, Texas, Ann would never have let me hug her in front of a crowded café. We didn't walk when we were in love — we skipped. We said hello to strangers and we laughed at nothing at all, only because it struck us both funny at the same time.

After many more dates, when I thought she accepted the fact I was not only a great writer but also a great lover, I invited her over to the Hôtel des États-

Unis to meet my friends.

Everyone in the bar was gracious enough, but my mind wasn't on the conversation. I finally got my nerve up and asked her if perchance she would like to see the room that had inspired my best writing. She made the usual excuses for not taking me up on my offer, and I kept trying to persuade her why visiting someone's room in an authentic Polish hotel in Paris was akin to a religious experience. Fortunately, common sense prevailed. I am not telling tales out of school. Ann wrote about us making love in her own book, *Seems Like Yesterday*, which reveals the story of our life in Paris. Her version is somewhat different from mine.

I interrupted her during the book to correct the gross errors, but it did me no good. All the women who have read the story preferred to accept Ann's version, and not mine.

I was surprised that she was not impressed with my room, since as Gertrude Stein would probably have said, "A bed is a bed is a bed is a bed."

An incident in the early morning spoiled our affair. The French police were constantly making the rounds of

151

the smaller Left Bank hotels, checking for illegal immigrants. The knock on the door came at three A.M. When Ann heard the word "Police," she ducked under the covers, shaking. I opened the door slightly. A uniformed *flic* said "Passports." I produced mine, which he inspected. Then he asked if there was anyone else in the room. I nodded my head and said, "Yes, but she is an American student and she left her passport at home." The *flic* chuckled, and said, "Tell her the next time she stays overnight to bring her identity papers with her."

Ann cried until dawn. I decided not to ask her if she would come back. Despite the knock on the door, we continued to see each other all the time frequenting restaurants, bars, and night clubs.

The police interruptions at the hotel persuaded me it was time to move. Through the grapevine I found a studio on the top floor of a building at 24, rue du Boccador, just off the avenue George-V. Living in the building were writers Irwin Shaw and Theodore White; a wealthy entrepreneur named Theo Benahume, who had introduced the Reynolds ballpoint pen to France; and a French producer named Raoul Lévy, who produced the Brigitte Bardot films. We were a merry band, and we went in and out of each other's apartments all the time without knocking or ringing doorbells.

Irwin Shaw has been one of the heroes in my life. He was a big bear of a man who laughed a lot, drank even more, and lavished much-needed encouragement on young writers. His novel *The Young Lions* had been a smash, and he was a literary godfather to dozens of American writers in Paris. Everyone felt better for being in his company. One of Irwin's most wonderful features was that he never had anything bad to say about a young person's writing. He wasn't as charitable about Hemingway or Norman Mailer, but where youth was concerned, he read our manuscripts and raved about our work, at the same time gently making suggestions. When Irwin praised our writing, it was as if we had made the front page of *The New York Times Book Review*.

Irwin had an agent named Irving Lazar who had made him rich. But Shaw paid a price for this. When he moved to Europe, the critics in the United States refused to take him seriously. They resented the fact he had exchanged a life in Brooklyn for a chalet in Klosters, Switzerland. I don't believe Irwin ever got any serious praise for the novels and short stories he wrote abroad — despite the fact that a great deal of his work was as good as anything being produced by the New York writers of the same period. Shaw was bitter about this, but he enjoyed the good life and had no intention of giving it up for anything.

When he was dying of cancer, I wrote and told him that I loved him very much.

Irwin attracted beautiful women, and his wife, Marion, a vivacious actress, did not like it one bit. One night, at a cocktail party, Marion thought Irwin was making a play for one of the guests. The woman was walking across the living room with a drink when Marion stuck out her foot and tripped her. She went flying, as did her drink, and Marion, with a poker face, said, "Oh dear, I'm terribly sorry. I just don't seem to know what to do with my feet anymore." The other wives at the party awarded Marion the Legion of Honor.

Teddy White had written *Thunder Over China* and would achieve further fame with *The Making of the President* series. He was small, wore thick glasses, and had a constant mischievous smile on his face. He was a brilliant reporter and as knowledgeable as any American on European politics. His only fault was that he had a tendency to be long-winded when he expounded on what the Russians were going to do to Turkey, when no one had asked him. But we found him a delightful person to share a meal with, or a living room couch. Teddy rarely held grudges, but he never forgave me for holding up the elevator on the fifth floor of the apartment building while he was trying to take his pregnant wife, Nancy, to the hospital to have a baby. I explained to him time and time again to no avail: "It wasn't me, Teddy — every time I pushed the Down button, the elevator went up."

I was still having to send Ann back to her French family in taxis after she visited my studio. Then luck smiled on me. The maid's room next to my studio was vacated, and I talked her into moving in. It was a very sensible arrangement. Her room was much smaller than mine, but when we were on friendly terms I would share my studio with her. When she got mad at me, I climbed out on my balcony, which connected with hers, and attempted to get into her room through her window. I had a collection of hats I had bought in the flea market, including those of a French general, a Berlin fireman, and a derby, which the owner assured me had once been owned by the head of British Intelligence. When Ann locked me out, I would put on one of my hats and appear in my underwear at her window reciting poetry from a book titled *Best Loved Poems of the American People.* There was a poem for every occasion, including "Inspiration," "Patriotism," and "Forgiveness." The one that worked the best for me was "Be the Best of Whatever You Are" by Douglas Malloch.

Here's part of it:

If you can't be a pine on the
*   top of a hill,*
Be a scrub in the valley
*   — but be*
The Best little scrub by
*   the side of the hill;*

Be a bush if you can't
be a tree.
If you can't be a bush be
a bit of the grass,
And some highway
happier make;
If you can't be a muskie
then just be a bass —
But the liveliest bass
in the lake!

The poem never failed to break Ann up and she would let me in.

As far as our pals were concerned, we were in a commitment situation. I didn't date other women and she didn't date other men. We saw each other every evening, and our friends never invited one without the other. What I liked the most about the arrangement was that Ann never brought up the subject of marriage. What I didn't like was that all our mutual friends did. There was a conspiracy amongst all to make us legal. I preferred the status quo, because I was in no position financially or psychologically to take on a wife. My ace in the hole was that I was Jewish and Ann was Catholic, and there wasn't a priest in all of Europe who would agree to marry us, unless I joined the Knights of Malta as a stable boy and enlisted in the Crusades on their ride to Jerusalem.

Everyone nosed into my business. One was Lauren (Betty) Bacall. After two years of living in sin (happily, I might add), Ann was threatening to go home, and told Betty she was tired of sleeping in a room next to me in what I considered utter bliss. Bacall, sounding just like Bacall, said something like, "Don't go. Nail him to the wall."

The next thing I received was an ultimatum. Ann did the speaking, but they were Bacall's words. "Since you don't want to marry me, I am going back to the States."

What I resented even more than Ann's lack of understanding was that she was forcing me to make an emotional decision, which is something I have hated to do. When I'm in a tight spot, I always start to upchuck. It's painful as hell, because most of it is dry heaving. That's what I did for several days before I went down to Cartier's and bought Ann an engagement ring. She was very happy. I had my doubts. I was concerned about the mixed marriage, the reaction of my father and sisters, and my career, which was just taking off. While I wore a smile in public, I kept heaving privately in the sink in my room.

In *Leaving Home*, I told the story of my childhood in an attempt to explain my reactions to certain situations. I had always been a loner. Because of my foster-home background and being deprived of a normal family existence, the idea of having a family of my own was as frightening as anything I could imagine. I saw myself as an uncle, but not as a husband and father. This was my way of avoiding pain. And the more I thought about the responsibility and taking on such alien emotions as love, the more I upchucked and wanted to escape.

What I planned to do was spend my life entertaining the crowd. I needed constant applause. I would go from one gathering to another, making new friends and new fans. Childhood wounds were too deep, and I was fearful of letting anyone get too close to me. I was a mess.

I wasn't hiding my emotions too well, because Ann got the message that I didn't want to go through with the marriage. She was very mad and threw her engagement ring back at me. I retrieved it and returned it to Cartier's. She told me she was going back to the U.S., but I asked her for a second chance, suggesting that we try our luck in Luxembourg. An American woman, Willa Amidon, who lived in a town called Echternach thought that we could cut through the red tape there. Echternach has a St. Vitus Day festival, when everyone dances all day long in the village streets to ward off the disease. So Ann and I went and we danced for fourteen hours, and although we didn't contract the disease, we didn't make any headway with our marriage plans, either. The good people of Luxembourg had no interest in two Americans who wanted to get married in their country. Publicly, I was disgusted with the red tape — privately, I was relieved.

Then I was blindsided by a completely unexpected source. Singer Lena Horne, with whom we used to hang out in a bar called La Calavados, across from the Hôtel George-V, heard the story of our trying to get married, and for no reason at all got involved. Lena said, "I know a priest in London who will marry anyone."

"What's his name?" I asked, my voice cracking.

"Father Milne. I'll call him tomorrow. He's at Westminster Cathedral."

I said "Wouldja?" I thought to myself, "Lena, I think you are the most wonderful singer in the world — why are you screwing up my life?"

The next night, she said, "It's all set. One of you is going to have to reside in England for two weeks to make it legal."

And so it came to pass that I went over to London to confront the sainted Father Milne. "I want to get married," I told him.

"No problem," he responded.

"Wait," I told him. "I'm Jewish and she's Catholic."

"No matter," he said. "As long as you're not a Protestant."

When the news of our pending marriage reached American shores, there was a great deal of head-shaking and tears in Warren, Pennsylvania, and in Forest Hills. A mixed marriage sounds easy in *Abie's Irish Rose*, but it isn't so wonderful in real life. I discussed with Abe Burrows what to tell my father. He said, "Tell him the following story. A Jewish boy goes to his mother and says,

'Mama, I'm going to marry a Gentile girl.' She says, 'Don't tell your Uncle Harry, since he goes to temple every morning — and you shouldn't say anything to your sister Maggie, because she doesn't have a stomach for mixed marriages — and be a good boy not to speak of it to your father, since he has a bad heart. As for me, you have my blessing, because I'm going to stick my head in the oven as soon as I finish dinner.' "

I did tell my father the story when I came home. He didn't laugh. But in his view I was the wild one, so why should he be surprised if I married a shiksa?

My most serious antagonist was a Father Bauer in Warren, and he was my mother-in-law's best friend. He was against mixed marriages. What he was really in favor of was complete control of his flock.

In fairness, I have to say that in spite of the roadblocks before the marriage, Ann's entire family accepted me and I had no trouble because of the religious differences. In fact, when I came home to Warren with Ann, her mother loved to show us off. The word went out that we were staying there, and relatives and friends kept popping into the house on one pretext or another. The fact that we lived in Paris was big for Warren, and they were all dying for news of Charles de Gaulle and Maurice Chevalier. And my family liked Ann as soon as they met her. My father was particularly charmed by her. Ann and I had some terrible rows over the years, but none of them was over religion.

The wedding took place on October 11, 1952, first in Westminster Cathedral and then in Caxton Hall. A woman named Norma Geer, who was fashion designer for the Celanese Corporation, and a client of Ann's, gave us a wedding reception at Claridge's. In attendance were such school chums as Al Hix from USC, harmonica player Larry Adler, Gene Kelly with his daughter Kerry, John Huston, José Ferrer, Ambassador Perle Mesta, producer Sam Spiegel, Clem Brown, and many other friends.

Ann and I agreed that this was quite a fairy-tale wedding for two kids from Warren and Queens — one Catholic, the other Jewish — married in London at Westminster Cathedral with their reception at Claridge's, the snootiest hotel in the city, while Gene Kelly danced with the bride and Rosemary Clooney toasted the groom.

When the reception was over, Ann and I retired to our hotel room. Ann changed into a white silk nightgown given to her by Balmain. I waited until she was in bed, and then came out of the bathroom in my underwear and a doorman's hat which I had borrowed. I proceeded to read from the *Best Loved Poems of the American People:*

GET A TRANSFER
If you are on the
  Gloomy Line,
    Get a transfer.
If you're inclined to fret
  and pine,
    Get a transfer.
Get off the track of doubt
  and gloom,
Get on the Sunshine Train
  — there's room —
    Get a transfer.
If you're on the Worry Train,
    Get a transfer.
The Cheerful Cars are
  passing through,
And there's lots of room
  for you —
    Get a transfer.

Ann was laughing so hard, we never did make love.

We went to Majorca for our honeymoon and finally returned to Paris, where for fourteen years we lived happily ever after.

Many years later, when Ann wrote her book, she summed up the marriage. "Still, I have never taken him or our marriage for granted, and often under his more humorous messages is a hard kernel of truth. On our first anniversary he gave me a painting he had commissioned from a *Herald Tribune* artist: two cherubs flying through a field of hearts and flowers trailing a banner with the words 'Can this marriage be saved?' On our fifth wedding anniversary, he gave me a $500 check and a card saying, 'Each year of our marriage has been worth $100 to me. I'm running away from home; don't try to find me, I'm re-enlisting in the Marines under a false name. Please explain to the kids. I was never meant to be married anyway. We had a lot of laughs and I think we should be grateful. I hope we can still be friends.' A few years later, my anniversary flowers came with a note, 'I don't care if we are married, we still seem to be living in sin.'

"And on our twenty-second anniversary, 'There are twenty-four roses — twenty-two for when it was legal — two when it wasn't.'

"And on our silver anniversary, tucked into a pile of presents, was Art's passionate tribute — 'It only seems like twenty-four.' "

Ann presented me with a silver frame on our twenty-fifth anniversary. In it were printed my remarks from the same book:

"Every once in a while, I think about Paris. I hope at this very moment that some young American boy is standing out on the balcony in a top hat knocking on his girl's window and asking her if he can come in. And I hope she lets him in and finally blackmails him into marrying her by saying if he doesn't she'll go home. And if that poor chap is reading this, I can tell him from experience, after you get over upchucking it isn't a bad life at all."

After forty years of marriage, Ann and I separated in 1992. During the last ten years, we seemed to drift further and further apart. When a marriage fails, both sides examine what went wrong. I think that when we first married, I needed Ann for almost everything except the column. Her role was clearly defined. She took care of me, and I, in turn, made sure that she had everything she wanted. We were very social, our love life was just fine, and we laughed a lot.

As the children left home, several things happened. I had two clinical depressions for which I was hospitalized. Ann had a very severe heart attack and subsequent bypass surgery. Our communication changed — things that I thought were funny failed to amuse her. I spent more and more time on the telephone telling others my news but not sharing this with Ann. I was also in therapy, and changing in terms of the needs Ann provided me. Toward the end of our marriage, the only thing she could do for me was cook me dinner. Then I would disappear into my study to write.

It was a lonely time for both of us. Finally the situation became so painful that Ann said she hated it when I came home, and I said I hated coming home.

The original separation caused tremendous bitterness, and as time went on, Ann finally decided to get a divorce to begin her own life. Then tragedy struck. Before the divorce proceedings were started, she contracted lung cancer, which spread. The doctors pronounced her illness terminal and she spent one year suffering, much of it in bed. Joel, our son, quit his job to take care of her.

At first her anger was such that she would have nothing to do with me. Joel and her doctor, Michael Newman, who was also our closest friend in Washington, were forbidden to discuss her health with me.

Joel and I would walk along the canal in Georgetown. He was in a terrible predicament. I would ask, "How long does she have?" In order not to violate her trust, he would say, "I read an article in *Newsweek* which said that people with a certain type of lung cancer can survive for six or eight months."

During this time, the bond between Joel and me grew ever stronger. I needed him more than he needed me.

An Irish priest named Father Michael Kennedy was instrumental in opening the door for me, concerning Ann. He persuaded her that keeping me out when I wanted to come in was hurting her. So did Kay Graham and Eunice Shriver.

Finally she agreed. Her sisters were taking care of her at the time. I was invited for dinner. I heard later that she said to her sisters, "He probably won't even bring me a present."

As soon as I rang the bell, the three sisters were all standing at the door. They didn't look at me — they looked down at my hand. I was carrying a teddy bear. There was a sigh of relief and I was asked in.

The dinner went well, and Ann allowed me to come back into her life, and I was there every day. I discovered she was happiest talking about our days in Paris. I told her I was going to bring the book of poems and read them to her, as I had on her balcony. She looked at me with an impish smile, and said, "Don't you dare."

Once, near the end, she asked me, "Do you have a girl?"

I said, "No."

"That's good," she said. "You may not be much, but you're all I've got."

In those last visits, we revived some

of the magic of our marriage. We both reveled in how glorious those Paris years had been, and how lucky we were to have experienced them.

Ann lived her last days as she did all her life. She never let on to anyone how much she was hurting. She always had something funny to say to callers. Once she started to pick on me about something minor, and I said, "Don't do that. You'll only get mad at me and feel lousy again." A smile came on her face, and she said, "I guess you're right."

During those months of her illness, I realized again what a remarkable woman she was. She wore a mask to make sure no one would see her except at her most accommodating. She was very smart and very well read, and all her friends, even when she was very sick, kept calling her to tell her their hard-luck stories.

We could not have survived the way we were, but the years in Paris had been good — very, very good — and I wouldn't trade them for anything.

On our return from Majorca in October 1952, we found a beautiful one-bedroom apartment. It had an enormous wood paneled living room, a dining room, bedroom, and a kitchen. It was located on the quai d'Orsay. The price was right and it was perfect for newly-weds. Most Parisians have to be married for years before they get a chance to live on the Seine.

A word about French apartments. There never have been enough good ones. The price controls from World War II were still in existence, and woe to the politician who suggested they be removed. So most Paris flats rented for $50, $100, or $200 a month. The only way a landlord could make any money was to sell the lease to another party for $15,000 or $30,000. It was called key money, and permitted the renter to remain in the apartment at the frozen rate.

One landlord story I particularly enjoyed concerned our friends the Nolans, who agreed to pay an exorbitant rent of $2,000 a month because the owner had decorated his walls with an Utrillo, a Dufy, a Renoir, and other paintings, as well as sketches by Rembrandt and da Vinci. After Nolan signed the lease, he held a cocktail party for all his friends to show off the paintings. An art expert from the Louvre was one of the guests, and he went through the rooms, pointing at each painting and screaming, "Fake, fake, fake. By God, there isn't a real painting in the bunch."

Another housing story concerned a friend who answered an advertisement for an apartment on the Seine. The lady took him out on the balcony and pointed to the river. "In the morning you see the barges going up the river as the sun rises. At noon you see the children playing on the Quai and lovers stroll by. In the evening, as the sun sets, the barges come down the river and — it's so beautiful — it's so beautiful — it's so beautiful — I will never rent it. Get out of here. And don't ever bother me again."

Thanks to the *Trib* classifieds, we found a manservant who cooked, cleaned, and bowed to us at all times. His name was Tsien. We thought he was Chinese, but it turned out he was Korean. But it didn't matter, because Tsien cooked Chinese — great Chinese. He told us at the time of his hiring he had formerly owned a Chinese restaurant. We gave him a meager salary and a room in the top of the apartment house and our lives were blessed.

Little did I know that this kind, gentle man would cost me a fortune. Whenever we had a dinner cooked by Tsien, all the guests raved. We were the hit of Paris, because most of our friends ate French food every night, and Chinese cuisine turned out to be a real treat.

The only trouble with this was that they kept saying to Tsien, "You ought to open a Chinese restaurant."

Tsien, who claimed to know no English, understood every word they were saying. One day, he came to me and said he would like to open a restaurant. I did not want to lose him, so I said, with a grin, "Of course you do — and when you find a location, I will help you."

It was his turn to smile. "I have."

I was stuck. To buy the key money for the lease and get it furnished and ready for business, I budgeted $30,000. It cost $50,000. I raised the money amongst my friends — Irwin Shaw, Anatole Litvak, Darryl Zanuck, John Huston, Clem Brown, and others.

A full share cost $2,000 — a half share $1,000. Charlie Torem, a distinguished American lawyer who handled

173

everyone from J. Paul Getty to the Aga Khan, was in charge of the legal details. He set it up so that as president, I was the only one in the company that could go to jail.

After terrible fights with the decorator, we opened up Chinatown on the rue François I er. It could seat a maximum of thirty-six people. The kitchen was in the basement, and assistant cooks working for Tsien kept collapsing from the heat.

My intention was to pay off the investors and then talk them into giving the restaurant to Tsien. It wasn't easy. While most of the partners were millionaires, they treated their investment as if it was a General Motors gilt-edge bond. We were paying off at $40 a month to each person. This did not stop Darryl Zanuck's aide de camp from calling me monthly to find out why the check was late.

The headaches from the restaurant were endless. Once, Zanuck, with his girlfriend of the moment, couldn't get a table when he walked in. He was so humiliated he called me at home that night to complain about his treatment, and to inform me he would never go there again.

Another time, lawyers from Pepsi-Cola chairman Al Steele's estate came to see me in Paris to inspect Chinatown's books. I showed them what I had, which wasn't much. They said they found the numbers very unsatisfactory.

I said, "Look. You guys are going to write off your whole trip to Europe by saying you met me to discuss the Chinatown investment. If you don't like what I've shown you, you can get the hell out of here."

Mike Todd, the producer of *Around the World in 80 Days*, took over the restaurant, against my wishes, to give a party for his film. We couldn't handle it, but Todd insisted and ran up a tab of $4,000. At two in the morning, Mike and Elizabeth Taylor were saying goodbye. Tsien was standing there with the bill. Mike told him, "Bring it around at eleven o'clock tomorrow morning to the Meurice hotel."

As Elizabeth kissed me on the cheek, she whispered, "We're leaving at seven."

After they had gone, I grabbed the bill and went to the Meurice, where I dozed in a chair in the lobby until six in the morning and then went upstairs to Mike's suite. When he opened the door, I said, holding the bill up, "I just came to say good-bye."

All Mike could say, as he counted out the francs, was, "Son of a bitch."

We never paid back the entire restaurant investment. At the same time, I didn't go to jail. In due course, Tsien died and we gave up our shares. I should have known when he started working for Ann and me — washing, ironing, and cooking and playing the role of the perfect manservant — that he was too good to be true. Every once in a while, Ann and I would say to each other, "At least we had him for a little while."

Things were moving along nicely for me on the *Trib.* Among the columns running in the newspaper was one called "Mostly About People."

It was being written as a diary by five reporters and an editor named Mike Horton. Little by little, the number of writers for the column dwindled until there were none. A reporter named Robert Yoakum and I offered to take on the column for an extra $50 each a week. Eric said okay, and the two of us wrote it, alternating items.

It worked fine for several months, when one day Yoakum went out to do a piece on the World Veterans — an anti-war organization founded by Alfred Vanderbilt. The idea was to unite all veterans who had fought in World War II to prevent another war.

Yoakum came back with a job offer to be their PR man for $10,000 a year.

He bequeathed me the column, which I was happy to write myself.

There was no shortage of people to write about. In the early fifties, Paris was a must for tourists and big-shot Americans. The grand tour was London, Paris, and Rome, and Americans from all walks of life were welcome, particularly if they carried traveler's checks. The dollar was the key to every country's kingdom. There were large discounts for American currency. There was a black market in French francs and Italian lire. It was a golden age for Americans, and one we may never see again.

As residents of Paris, we all had our personal money changers. Mine was named Pop and he had an apartment on the Champs-Elysées. Pop not only gave the top price for the dollar, but he was much easier to deal with than the French banks, which required their cashiers to fill out hundreds of forms before changing the dollars into francs.

I took favored visitors to Pop, and they were as impressed with getting a higher rate for their dollar as they were with the Louvre Museum. My friends from Hollywood and New York — people who had millions — still were ecstatic to beat the exchange rate for one hundred dollars' worth of francs.

While Pop was a legitimate black-market money dealer, there were many who had no morals or ethics and actually shortchanged their customers. A man would sidle up to you in the street and say, "I give you six hundred francs for the dollar." (This at the time when the official rate was 395.) Tourist greed would immediately take over. The money changer would say, "Follow me." He would take you into an alley and a hallway, and you would hand him $500 in traveler's checks. He would count out the francs and then you would count them out — and then he would count them out again.

Then he would shake hands and walk away. After he had disappeared, you would count one more time and discover that he had shorted you $100 in francs. For days, you would wonder how he had pulled it off.

Because of our solid currency, not all Americans behaved kindly toward the French. The phrase "the Ugly American" kept popping up. Some Americans constantly accused the Parisians of cheating them. There were snide remarks about French toilet paper, and French money that looked like Kleenex. Worst of all, the Americans patronized Parisians and treated them like poor relations.

These days the American dollar looks more like Kleenex than the French franc. Unfortunately, American tourists who now come to Paris arrive on package tours, and since they hardly make a dent on the commerce of the town, they are no longer even the butt of French jokes.

As I have said, everybody came to Paris in the fifties. The *Herald Tribune* building was de rigueur on the sightseeing tour. On nights when I was escorting Danny Kaye, or Fred Allen, or

Ed Sullivan around Paris, I took them to the *Tribune* after dessert. The staff may not have been impressed by the visitors, but the visitors were extremely impressed by the staff.

I would walk into the city room around eleven thirty at night and say, "Hey, everyone. This is Humphrey Bogart." No one bothered to look up from their copy. If, on the other hand, I walked in and said, "Hi, this is Jane Russell," they would mutter something polite.

I played host to weird people like David Schine and Roy Cohn. Schine owned theaters and Roy Cohn was a young lawyer for Senator Joseph McCarthy. Cohn and Schine arrived in Paris on an investigation of Reds in the State Department. It was their first trip to Europe, and the press was dying to have a go at them.

A few weeks before their arrival, I had purchased a West German wire recorder, which you wore underneath your arm in a holster. It also came with a wristwatch which served as a microphone. I was assured by the sales person that all the spies in Europe had them. I plunked down $350 because I knew it would be terribly useful in my work.

In those days, the international press corps was a very eclectic group, consisting of well-oiled Americans, British, and other nationalities. They were our "foreign correspondents" and they wore raincoats and enjoyed a very luxurious life, because their newspapers thought they were hot stuff who knew what they were talking about.

Before the conference began, I said, "Hey, I have this wire recorder and we'll get these bastards on it so they can't deny they said something. You don't have to take notes. Just give me a good seat."

They did, and when Cohn and Schine came in, I had my arm out and my watch practically sticking in their nostrils. It was a rancorous press conference, and neither side backed down. But Cohn and Schine did say enough outrageous things to confirm how frightening two loose anti-Communist cannons can be.

When the show was finished, the reporters rushed me over to the Hotel Crillon. I took the wire recorder out of its holster, turned on the button, and it went "Screeeeeeeeeeeech." There was nothing on the wire but a horrendous noise. I hadn't recorded a word.

Some correspondents discussed setting fire to me at the table. Others thought it would be better to drop me from the top of the Eiffel Tower. They spent hours trying to recall the conference as it had taken place. Even when I picked up the check for their drinks, they still wanted to kill me.

There is a happy ending to this story. A month after the incident, a young man named Jack Cahn came into my office. He told me his father owned a string of movie theaters and resorts in Florida, but he wanted to go into the newspaper business and was wondering if I had any tips for him.

I reached into my drawer for a cigar and saw the recorder. Then I said, "Well, if you're serious about being a reporter, I assume you have a German wire recorder."

He said, "No, I don't."

"Then you haven't much chance of getting into the game."

"Do you know where I can get one?" he said.

"I'll see what I can do," I told him.

"Come back tomorrow."

When he came back, I sold him my wire recorder for $350 — the same price I had paid for it. I wish I could tell you that young man turned out to be another Woodward and Bernstein, but it's not so. I got a note from him six months later, telling me he had gone into his father's resort business.

Years later, I was in Florida, staying at a hotel in Sarasota with my family. Damned if the Cahns didn't own the hotel, and damned if the father wasn't so grateful to me for selling his son a German wire recorder that he picked up the hotel tab for the week.

I was sorry none of my friends at the Crillon could see how that recorder finally paid off.

Since my desk was strategically located by the door, I became the city room's doorkeeper. I kept daytime hours, so there was rarely anyone else there in the mornings and early afternoons.

One day, a very attractive girl in an angora sweater, plaid skirt, and saddle shoes stopped by. She said her name was Beth and she had just graduated from Mount Holyoke and was hoping to get a job on the *Herald Tribune.* I told her, as I did every job-seeker, that there were no jobs on the *Tribune*, but we chatted about her ambition to become a writer.

Six months later, I was walking by the Café Flore, and I heard someone yell, "Hey, Art." I turned toward the voice but did not recognize the face. The eyes had a heavy coating of mascara, the lips were heavily rouged, and the hair was black and stringy. She said, "Don't you remember me? I'm Beth."

"Of course you are," I said.

Then I asked, "What have you been doing?"

"I'm writing porn books for the Olympia Press."

"That's good," I said. "I read them all the time. Are they hard to write?"

"They were in the beginning, because Girodias said I was too explicit. So I had to tone the sex stuff down a little. But it's not that difficult. The formula is to have something erotic on every *other* page."

"How much do you get paid?"

"Five hundred dollars, but no royalties."

She had a long cigarette holder that

kept getting in my face. "I'm proud of you," I told her. "You're the first person who came into my office who landed a good job without help from your parents."

The man she worked for, Michel Girodias, published not only porn books — that kept landing him in the French courts for obscenity — but good writers such as Henry Miller, Terry Southern, Frank Harris, and William Burroughs. But he was also famous for getting many well-known authors to write under fictitious names, either for money or for kicks.

A large portion of our Paris life was spent entertaining visiting firemen, mostly from the United States. It seemed that as soon as someone announced he or she or both were going to Paris, someone said, "You have to look up our good friends, the Buchwalds," even though they weren't good friends of ours at all.

Many of the people we met were very interesting, very successful, and very rich, and whereas they wouldn't have seen us in the United States, they sought us out in Paris in hopes we would spend an evening with them.

Once we went to dinner with Norman and Buff Chandler, and at that time she was raising money for the Music Center in Los Angeles. "Young man," she said, "I want you to find out what hotel Jean Paul Getty is staying in and what his room number is."

I said, "You'll never get any money out of Jean Paul Getty."

She replied stiffly, "I don't need your advice. Just get me the information."

I found out he was staying at the Hôtel George-V, in apartment 567. I passed on the intelligence to Mrs. Chandler.

Years later, Getty told me the rest of the story. At eight thirty in the morning, Buff started hammering at his door, shouting, "Paul, I know you're in there. I just want to talk to you for five minutes."

Still dazed, the oil magnate told me, "She walked away with my check for fifty thousand."

I had one call from a gentleman who said he had brought me some wonderful Havanas. I invited him for lunch at Fouquet's. As soon as we sat down, he said, "Here are your cigars," and offered me two. Then he told me that he had been sent by a mutual acquaintance named Al White.

"How's Al?" I asked.

"I don't exactly know Al," he said. "I know a friend of Al's, and when Al heard through my friend that I was going to Paris, he said, 'Be certain to look up Buchwald.' "

As we ate lunch, I got an idea. "I want you to do me a favor. Since you don't know Al, I want you to go to his office with a letter from me. I will write that you are a Frenchman visiting New York for the first time, and I would appreciate it if he could take you to *My Fair Lady.* I'm also going to suggest that Al's wife take your wife to Bloomingdale's. All I ask is that you report to me what happened."

He agreed, and I delivered the letter to him. Two months later, I got a cryptic note from the visiting fireman. All it said was, "I delivered the letter, and his secretary said he was too busy to see me."

We had our own little mafia in Paris and we saw each other several times a week. It included Alain and Margie Bernheim. (Years later, Alain and I would both sue Paramount for breach of contract over a film called *Coming to*

America, starring Eddie Murphy.) Alain and I often sat at Fouquet's, which was patronized by movie people. Alain was a literary and motion picture agent, and we were constantly dining with producers who had no chance of ever getting a motion picture off the ground but nevertheless were full of charm.

At that time in the fifties, we both had mothers-in-law, and one year they happened to be in town at the same time. Every morning, they checked in with each other to find out what their sons-in-law had done for them.

One Sunday evening, I took my mother-in-law and Ann to the garden at the Plaza-Athénée for a quiet dinner. We were the only ones there when Gary Cooper walked in alone. We invited him to join us. A few minutes later, Ingrid Bergman arrived by herself and we invited her to sit down. (Years later it dawned on me that something was going on between Cooper and Bergman.) Then Anatole Litvak, the director, joined us, with Bettina, the model, who was Aly Khan's girlfriend.

It was a merry table and we all had a ball, and my mother-in-law was in heaven.

The next morning, very early, she called up Mrs. Kessler, Margie's mother, and laid it on, relating a minute-by-minute description of the evening.

Alain called up an hour later and said, "What the hell are you doing to me? You're making my life miserable."

"It was all an accident. I didn't expect to see anyone at the Plaza on Sunday night. What did you say to your mother-in-law when she told you what happened to us?"

He said, " 'Why are you complaining? I introduced you to Paulette Goddard,' and she said, 'Yes — you start and *stop* with Paulette Goddard.' "

The most sought-after American star in Paris was Orson Welles. Everyone wanted to do a film with him. Orson was not that interested in their projects, but he loved to eat, so he always accepted invitations for lunch or dinner to "discuss the deal." I was at a few of these meals. Orson had an incredibly deep voice and when he ordered a rare $150 bottle of Lafitte-Rothschild, he would roar with laughter, as if it was all a joke he was sharing with his host.

One of the most dangerous parts of

taking out visitors to Paris was that some people were very tight and refused to pick up the tab. They seemed to think that I was on an unlimited expense account — or worse still, they never had any intention of picking up the check. Ann used to get furious particularly when we didn't even know the people who were sent to us by friends, and we got stuck with the bill.

I wasn't the only one with visiting-American stories, of course. One of my best friends during those years was a French doctor named Jean Dax, who took care of many of the Americans in Paris. Jean was not only our doctor but a buddy. Occasionally, without using names, he would tell us some of his more amusing medical adventures. He spoke perfect English, so many of the fancy hotels used him to treat their guests.

One day, he received a call from the Hôtel George-V. The caller was in hysterics, and claimed that her husband was having a heart attack. When Jean showed up, the wife, who was from New York, was yelling at her husband, "You work all the time. You never had time for your family, you never had time for me. And now you're having a heart attack and you're going to die and leave me a widow."

Jean said to the wife, "Would you please let me examine him?" He had a portable cardiograph. After the examination, Jean said, "He's not having a heart attack. He's just tired. I think he should stay in the hotel this weekend and get some rest."

The wife started yelling again. "We come to Paris once in a lifetime and we have to spend it in this stinking hotel room. A fine vacation I'm having!"

One of his other stories concerned a woman who called him from the Plaza-Athénée. She said she wanted to talk to Jean about her aunt. When he got to the room, the caller was waiting in the hall. The eighty-year-old aunt had lost her husband, Victor, six months ago. She refused to admit he was dead and insisted on "traveling" with him. The big problem was that the aunt claimed Victor would pay all the bills. Since there was no Victor, the niece was paying them and running out of money.

Dax asked how he fit in to all this.

The niece said she wanted Dax to certify that her aunt was incompetent and send her home. Jean explained that it took years of paperwork to do that. However, he went in to see the lady, who was very cheery, and introduced him to Victor. She also invited Jean to dinner at Maxim's. Jean went, and when the bill came, Victor did not make a grab for it, so Dax got stuck. He also went to lunch with her and got stuck for that.

Jean wracked his brain for a solution to the dilemma. He went back to the hotel room and asked the widow to step into the bedroom with him, so he could talk to her privately. There he said, "I don't like the way Victor looks."

The old lady said, "What's wrong?"

"It could be his heart. I wouldn't trust a French cardiologist when it comes to hearts. We're good with livers — but hearts belong to the Americans. Please get him back to America as fast as possible."

The old lady nodded, and in hours, she was packed and gone with her niece. When Dax told the story, a pained look appeared on his face. He said that he accompanied them to the airport, and on the off chance, he gave the old lady his bill for four days of

The boy from Queens, New York – the girl from
Warren, Pennsylvania. Paris was made for them.
(JAMES WHITMORE)

above: News of Truman's victory in 1948 shook Harry's New York Bar.

above right: Ursula was my secretary, nanny, and protector from evil French bureaucrats.

right: I always loved the fashion shows, because the models let me carry their boxes.
(SHAROK HATAMI)

right: Life was not what it seemed if you hung out in the dressing rooms of the Crazy Horse Saloon. (DOUGLAS KIRKLAND)

below: Many Frenchmen used to stop me on the street and demand to know why the dollar was strong and the franc was weak. (SHAROK HATAMI)

above: The way to prepare yourself for the running of the bulls in Pamplona was to drink a very good vintage Spanish wine.

right: I crashed the party of the decade in Venice as Louis XIV. Overnight, I became a member of the ruling elite.

right: According to Ernest Hemmingway, to be a great writer one had to go on safari and kill a large wild animal. He said it wasn't the name of one's publisher but the name of one's white hunter that impressed readers.
(JOE COVELLO)

below: Our Chrysler broke down in Poland, and we had to borrow an extra horse from a farmer to pull the car out of the snow.

above: Ingrid Bergman let me read all the hate mail she received after she ran away with Roberto Rossellini. That's when I fell in love with her.

below: Lunch with American gangster Lucky Luciano in Naples was always a treat and a privilege.

facing page, top left: Ann was very beautiful and became my most loyal cheerleader. (CARL PERUTZ, MAGNUM)

top right: We finally got married in London and made all our friends very happy. (ANDREY ANDERSSON)

bottom right: One of the great moments of my life in Paris was jamming with Duke Ellington and Louis Armstrong.

above: Our greatest gift from Paris was Joel, left, then
Connie and Jennifer. (MARK SHAW)
below: Leaving for America fourteen years later. There
was no good way to say good-bye.
(SHAROK HATAMI)

services. All she said was, "Thank you, Doctor. Victor will take care of it."

My flow of visitors was endless. One day a woman came in and said, "You went to USC, didn't you?"

I said I did.

"I want you to do something for the school. I want you to help me hang a banner over the Arc de Triomphe."

"What does it say?" I asked.

"Beat Stanford."

I said, "My God, but that's the Tomb of the Unknown Soldier."

She said, "No guts, huh?"

Two other visitors were Mr. Lew Swartout and his vice president, Charles Granville, who said they represented an American perfume company. They had come to Paris to promote their perfume Black Satin. Granville said that his people were sick and tired of the French believing that French perfume was the best, when they had never been exposed to American fragrances.

What they intended to do, said Swartout, was seed the clouds over Paris with a mixture of Black Satin and carbon dioxide. When it rained on the city, it would pour Black Satin.

Granville told me there were problems. The American ambassador to France, Douglas Dillon, refused to supply weather maps, and French authorities were silent on the project. Swartout said that the only encouragement so far had been that Senator Prescott Bush (George Bush's father) had cabled them: "Will put your idea in the *Congressional Record*, but suggest you get permission from the French before undertaking project." Swartout considered the cable a complete U.S. endorsement.

From my viewpoint, the whole scheme was too good to be true, and I went out to the airport to fly wing on the plane that was going to seed the cloud that would cause Black Satin to rain all over Paris.

I saw Swartout and the pilot disappear into a cumulus cloud. When we got back to the airport and returned to Paris, the streets were dry. But a half hour later — and I swear to this — Paris had the worst thunderstorm of the summer.

Swartout and Granville were dancing up and down. "We did it, we did it. Can't you smell it?"

"How do you know you are not smelling Black Satin on your clothes?" I asked.

"Don't you know the difference between perfume on your clothes and perfume raining down from the clouds?"

"I wish I did," I told them.

I called the American Embassy to see if they had smelled anything.

My contact said, "I'd rather not tell you what it is."

One afternoon, a writer-director named Don McGuire came in to see me. His wife was shopping and he was bored. "Let's go out and drive tourists crazy."

I was curious to find out what he had on his mind. So we walked over to the Champs-Elysées. Let me explain something here: Most people are very timid when they visit other countries, and will not question anything said to them.

We walked past a U.S. Army truck that was parked on the Champs. The driver was asleep. McGuire hit the door with his fist as hard as he could. The driver woke up with a start, and McGuire said, "If I ever catch you sleeping again, I'm going to ship your ass to Korea. Is that understood?"

The driver saluted and said, "Yessir." He sat at attention as we walked away. McGuire seemed pleased. We approached the Arc de Triomphe, and were just a block away when Don pointed to a tourist trying to take a photo of it. He was with his wife. McGuire walked up to him and, in a clipped military voice, said, "May I see your passport?"

The flustered tourist reached for his passport and handed it to McGuire. Don studied it carefully, comparing the photo with the man. Then he slapped the passport with his hand, and said, "Do you have permission to take a photograph of a military installation?"

The tourist replied in a trembling voice, "I, I didn't know it was a military installation."

"Well, for Christsakes — next time, ask."

Don handed the man's passport back to him, and we watched as he and his wife dashed away, trying to put as much distance between themselves and the Arc as possible.

Sometimes the visitors to the *Trib* were not as benign. Once I wrote an article in which I referred to Aly Khan as a Persian. This enraged an Iranian, who came into the office yelling and spitting at me that Aly Khan was not a Persian — he was a Pakistani. He demanded an apology, and I, of course, gave it to him.

There was pathos in some of the strangers who came in. I recall once a couple who had not heard from their daughter in two years, and wanted to know how to put an advertisement in the newspaper asking her whereabouts. "Myrna, we love you very much. Please contact us right away. Grandma is sick." I helped them place the ad, but I doubted it would bring results. Europe had its share of American runaways, and unless they wanted to come home the authorities did little to find them.

Myrna very likely saw the ad, though. The classified advertisements in the *Herald Tribune* were one of its most popular features. "Am looking for George who shared a sandwich with me on Trafalgar Square on April 1, 1943." — "For Sale: 1950 Pontiac, French tags, owner going back to the States." — "Will share apartment with another student in exchange for French tutoring." — "Anyone looking for 10,000 empty ammunition boxes, contact Floyd." — "Jeanette, Forget what happened in Helsinki. Let's start all over again."

Because of its slim size (sometimes only six pages), every item in the paper was read. The impact of the paper, plus its availability all over the Continent, made it the most unique publication of its kind. Time and time again, people have told me how it helped cure them of homesickness.

At the height of my career in Paris, I wrote for eighty-five newspapers. After I moved to Washington, my column appeared in 550. Yet I had an entirely different relationship with the reader in Paris than in the United States. I was confidant, friend, and family to the person who read me in the European edition. We had a chemistry and a connection that was meaningful. When I returned to the United States, I was simply one of many columnists available in a newspaper, and my role was far less personal. I was no longer family.

Publishers like Sam Newhouse of the Newhouse papers, and Otis Chandler of the *Los Angeles Times*, were amazed that we could turn out a newspaper with such a far-reaching circulation.

There were no computers and the presses belonged in a museum, yet the paper had a unique soul.

Where was Ann while I did my nightly fandango? She was either with me, or remained at home when she was too tired. She never raised any questions about the hours I kept or the countries I visited. It was part of the job. Besides, she had her own business in the beginning, and was busy promoting Dutch tulip bulbs, cognac, Celanese, and the French fashion industry.

How much of a living could she make as a PR lady in Paris with two partners — Maggie Nolan and Dorothy Schoenbrun? I never paid much attention, but the French tax people did.

Ann's accounts were high-flying names, but they didn't pay much. Her biggest coup as a PR person was to persuade the Eiffel Tower people, who were having the structure painted brown, to announce that they were painting it "cognac." Ann told them that it would be much better for France — and wouldn't cost them a franc. It was agreed, and was so successful that *Fortune* decided to do a story on the three girls. In order to hype the article, the writer said they made $50,000 a year. The French tax people, who apparently read *Fortune* from cover to cover, were amazed at how well the ladies were doing. So they sent two agents to their offices on the Champs-Elysées. Dottie Schoenbrun, the wife of CBS correspondent David Schoenbrun, sized up the men even before they flashed their identification, and grabbed the two company ledgers and took them into the bathroom, where she sat on them for an hour, while the tax people questioned Ann and Maggie.

Ann told me they hung around so long that her biggest fear was that one of the men would ask to go to the bathroom. Nobody knows how much they would have been fined if Dottie hadn't grabbed the books. When Jim Nolan heard the story, his only reaction was, "Well, at least she had some fiction to read on the toilet."

What made Ann furious was that I wouldn't touch one of her promotions in my column with a ten-foot pole. She said she didn't mind me ignoring the puff jobs, but she maintained I could at least say something nice about

Dutch tulip bulbs without compromising myself.

Ann's job gave her a lot to do, and she did it all to perfection.

While we were both doing what had to be done, we were also trying to make babies. Ann came from a family of eleven, and assumed the more children you had, the more successful the marriage would be. I had no objections, but for reasons we never clearly understood, Ann just couldn't get pregnant. We went for tests, and Dr. Lester Lipsitch at the American Hospital told me I had a low sperm count, but no medication was prescribed.

But we both wanted children and were prepared to do whatever was necessary to have a family. The subject of adoption came up several times, particularly when our friends told us about places in Europe where children were available.

On one occasion, Ann, who had been reading books on fertility, took her temperature and, according to her information, she decided that she was in a very fertile mode. She called me at noon in the office and told me to rush home. I did as she asked, and we hoped against hope that it was the right moment. Sadly, nothing happened. But the good side was that we had found a new way to spend our two-hour lunch.

While we were despairing, some friends living in Paris, the Cooneys, had adopted a child from a Dublin orphanage, and suggested that we might make a pitch there. The home was called St. Patrick's Guild, and it was run by nuns. We made our request, and after much paperwork with the Catholic Welfare League, we heard from the orphanage. They had selected a child for us. He was fourteen months old. The nuns sent along a photo of the baby boy, who was to become our first child. He turned out to be the most beautiful child either of us could have hoped for.

The nuns wrote that he would be ours in time, if all went well. It sounded too good to be true. There would be no walking up and down the hospital corridors in anticipation of a newborn baby. There would be no bedside scenes with an exhausted Ann holding a tiny, wrinkled infant. But, as I found out, adoption contains as much trepidation. You are taking full responsibility for a human being who is not your own. In the beginning, you go overboard not to do anything to upset the child. You give him too much food, you buy too many clothes, and if he cries or yells, you panic. I once made a speech to a group of adoptive parents, and I told them, "You really know your adopted child is yours when you decide he's as big a pain in the ass as every other kid on the block."

Receiving a photo of a baby in the orphanage, and actually getting him, were two very different things. There was a lot of red tape in Ireland, and that included getting someone to approve the adoption of a Catholic boy into a mixed marriage. For a long time, this issue caused anyone who had to stamp a paper in Dublin not to stamp one.

Finally, out of frustration, I said to Ann, "Let's go over and show up at the orphanage. They can't turn us down." We left on Saturday and arrived at the Dublin airport, where we told the taxi driver to take us to St. Patrick's Orphanage. When we arrived, we announced to the nun who we were and demanded to see "our son."

The nun said she had no idea what we were talking about.

This infuriated me, because the last thing I expected from a nun was to play games with us. I whipped out the photograph and said, "This is our son."

She responded, "We don't have anyone here resembling that child."

"Jesus," I said, without crossing myself, "do you think we made this up?"

"Wait a minute," the nun said. "This is St. Patrick's Home. You want St. Patrick's Guild. That's another orphanage across town."

We rushed out, hailed another taxi, and arrived at St. Patrick's Guild at five-thirty at night. This time, the nuns knew who we were, but they were most indignant that we had shown up before being given the green light.

The Mother Superior said, "If we show you Joseph, and then you can't have him, it will be a terrible disappointment to you."

"No, no," I assured her, lying through my teeth. "It won't bother us at all."

Ann also lied. "If we don't get him, we'll find somebody else."

The Mother Superior took us into a little playroom. Joseph was sitting on the floor, putting blocks together. He had blond hair and his complexion was very flushed. Later on, Ann told me that his appearance indicated that he wasn't getting enough fresh fruit and vegetables.

We walked up to him very slowly. Ann was crying. I was shaking. "Hi, son," I said. He didn't know what to make of us. Ann picked him up and I just kept patting him. It was his turn to cry. I don't think we stayed in the playroom for more than fifteen minutes.

We were escorted to the door. The Mother Superior said, "This is a very difficult case. There has been so much publicity about Irish children being turned over to Americans that the Foreign Office has stopped issuing passports. Besides that, there is some concern by the cardinal's office over the mixed-marriage situation. Please don't get your hopes up."

In her book, Ann's description of that first meeting is much better than mine. She wrote, "His face was flushed as if he had been running for hours. He had two or three layers of clothing on to ward off the cold of the building. He sat motionless on the floor and studied Art and me cautiously. Art said, 'Look at the red car we brought you.' Joseph's eyes solemnly followed the toy as Art pushed it back and forth. He smiled for the first time."

I told the Mother Superior that I thought Joseph was a very attractive boy. What I didn't say was that I was prepared to take on the cardinal, as well as the Irish prime minister, to get him out of St. Patrick's.

One of the biggest hurdles was obtaining a passport. Liam Boyd, the TWA public relations man in Dublin, had attended school with the foreign minister. In Ireland, the only way to get anything accomplished is if one friend calls another and says, "Listen, Brian, I need a small favor." (No one ever asks for a big favor.) Liam said to the foreign minister, "I have this American newspaper friend and we must have a passport for the child he is adopting here in Dublin, and the best to your missus."

The foreign minister came through in twenty-four hours.

Now we had to deal with the Church. Liam also had connections there, because the secretary to the cardinal was someone he went to the race track with.

In no time, we had an appointment with the cardinal himself. He was the major hurdle. Without his blessing, there was little chance of Joseph becoming our son.

On the morning of the audience, I was given my instructions by Ann.

"Be sure and kiss his ring," she said.

"I'll bite his entire finger off if you want me to," I told her.

"And for God's sake, let him do the talking."

"Don't worry. If he says Moses was a troublemaker, I'll say, 'Right.' "

We were ushered in. I kissed the ring, and the cardinal said, "How can I be sure Joseph will be raised Catholic?" I told the cardinal that since he had already been baptized a Catholic I had no problem with him being raised in the Catholic church. This seemed to please him very much. I replied, "I'll send him to Notre Dame or Holy Cross, and promise never to let him forget that he's a son of Ireland."

My lips had one more crack at the ring and we were out in the street, discussing whether we had passed the test or not. We had, because the next day we received a call from the Mother

Superior, telling us that the cardinal's office had telephoned saying everything was in order. It was all right for us to take Joseph with us on the following day.

We celebrated with Liam Boyd and a Dublin liquor distributor named Nora Fitzgerald, a friend of Liam's. The next morning, as soon as the stores opened, we went down to buy clothes, toys, and all the things excited parents assume a small child cannot do without.

When we showed up, the nuns had Joseph ready. We had already decided we were going to rename him Joel. His cheeks were red, and his eyes kept going back and forth between Ann and me. He held on to one nun as tight as he could, and she began to cry. After several tearful moments, she handed Joel to Ann, and he started wailing. We walked out of the Guild, but Joel didn't want to leave, and the dreadful thought occurred to me, "What right do I have to take him?"

We took a cab to the airport — each of us taking turns kissing him and touching him, in an attempt to reassure him that everything was going to be all right.

Forty years later, I still remember the taxi ride and my fear that at the last moment something would go wrong. Even when our plane took off. I was afraid that the Pope would overrule the cardinal and order the plane to land.

A few months after Joel came back to Paris with us, I flew to New York without Ann, and the designers Hannah Troy and Mollie Parnis gave me a baby shower. There were thirty-five women in attendance, and me. They dressed me in a baby bonnet, and photographed me with a cigar clenched between my teeth, opening presents to take back to Paris. They were all trying to outdo one another, and I ended up with some of the most expensive baby items available in New York. I was not only enjoying the idea of Joel, I took great pleasure in telling everyone that I was a father.

We lucked into our next child, Connie. We weren't looking for her at the time, but the gods were good to us. We found her during the most fortuitous junket I ever took.

I went to Spain at the invitation of United Artists to cover the making of a film titled *The Pride and the Passion*, a costume extravaganza directed by

Stanley Kramer and starring Cary Grant, Frank Sinatra, and Sophia Loren. The head publicity man was a friend named Richard Condon, who later became one of America's most successful authors with *The Manchurian Candidate* and *Prizzi's Honor.*

Condon turned me over to a pretty Spanish assistant named Conchita Stelli, who spoke flawless English and bubbled with energy.

During the course of a ride out to the set at Avila, I said to her, "Is it hard for foreigners to adopt children in Spain?" She said she didn't know, but she would find out. I told her we wanted a sister for our adopted son, Joel.

The next morning, I saw Conchita, and she said, as if I had asked for an autographed photo of Frank Sinatra, "I spoke to Mr. Mellado at the orphanage in Madrid. We have an appointment tomorrow."

Conchita knew how to flirt, and she convinced Mellado that Ann and I would be perfect parents for one of his children. The next morning, we went to a large, austere-looking building, which seemed like the Spanish equivalent of the Hebrew Orphan Asylum. After chatting for a few moments, Mellado asked the nurse to bring out the babies. I was very confused, since I had not seen many newborn ones and they all had crinkly faces.

While we were waiting for more foundlings, I asked Mellado if all the adoptions were of newborns.

"No. We have older children that we should get out of here. For example, this one." He showed me a photograph of a most beautiful child.

"Can we have her?" I asked.

"I imagine so. It's time for her to go."

Ann and I held hands when they brought Mathilda in. She was wearing a white linen dress and gold earrings. I noticed that her ears were pierced. Later, I discovered that the orphanage had only one linen dress and only one pair of earrings for their girl orphans to wear.

Mathilda was as suspicious of us as Joel had been, and we tried not to frighten her. Conchita was ecstatic over her, and kept purring soothing words to her in Spanish. We committed ourselves to her on the spot, and in time Mathilda became Conchita Mathilda Buchwald.

We ran into trouble, however, because Franco's Spain made life miserable for any person who applied for a passport. Once again, our friend Conchita saved the day. Having been rebuked by the passport authorities, Conchita went to the orphanage and asked for Connie to be dressed up again. Then we took her down to the passport office. Conchita marched in with Mathilda in her arms and shouted at one official after another, "You are depriving this beautiful child of a decent home in America because you won't give her documents. You should be ashamed of yourselves!"

The combination of the yelling Conchita, the beautiful Mathilda, and the sentimental instincts of the Spanish officials was too much, and we were given the passport. We got the hell out of Spain before Franco changed his mind.

We told Joel to expect a sister and he cleaned out his crib to make room for her. When we placed the children together for the first time, Joel hugged her tight. "Connie" was much more cautious, and looked at him as if to say, "Who on earth are you?"

Ann and I thought that our family was now complete, but a month later, our friend Dr. Lester Lipschitz, who had promised to be on the lookout for a baby for us, called and said that they might have one at the American Hospital in Paris.

He asked if we were interested, and we replied yes. He told us that according to French law he was obligated to persuade the biological mother to keep the child. Two weeks before giving birth, if she said that she didn't want it, we would give Lipschitz the name of a boy and a girl. When the baby was born, we were not to come to the hospital until the mother had left. Only then could we pick up the child, who, in this case, would be Jennifer Marie, and whose name would appear this way in the city hall register. At a later date, when she was legally adopted, they would add Buchwald. So there was no trace of the biological mother.

The baby was born on September 16, 1956. Ann called me at the *Trib* and told me the news. I remember turning to everyone in the city room and saying, "You're not going to believe this, but I just had a baby girl."

We brought Jennifer home in a basket two weeks later. By then we had moved to 52, rue de Monceau, across from the Parc Monceau, which featured prominently in the film *Gigi.*

So in no time we had gone from being a childless couple to a family of five. We added a nanny, a cook, and a cleaning lady. Where I got all the money to support everybody is something I have never figured out, but we paid the help and the rent and we still had francs left over to go dancing at Maxim's.

One day, when Ann was interviewing for a new maid, a woman walked in and Ann told her to be seated and asked to see her references. The woman replied that she had none with her. Ann asked, "Why are you wasting my time?" It turned out that the woman was not applying for the maid's position; she was doing a home study concerning Jennifer for the official French adoption agency. Fortunately, she had a sense of humor.

Until she was legally adopted, Jennifer had a guardian, who was supposed to visit once a week. He was a retired magistrate and he had very little else to do, so sometimes he came two or three afternoons a week, and we had to be very nice to him. After six months, the adoption was finalized and Jennifer was ours.

We never hid the fact from the children that they were adopted. One of the reasons was that everybody knew about them. Whenever the children walked into the living room, a visitor would say, "Now tell us which one is from Ireland, which one from Spain, and which one from France?"

I thought I should tell them the circumstances of their adoption every chance I could get, so I told their stories at bedtime. This backfired one day when Jennifer, who was six, said, "We're tired of that story. Why don't you tell us a real one?"

I never had any discomfort with adopting children. This is probably because I had such a checkered childhood of my own I did not put as much emphasis on "birth children" as other people did. This became a constant source of disagreement between Ann and myself, however. Although she was very happy with our three adopted children, she longed to have babies of her own. She often mentioned to me how she felt that she had failed in her maternal duties.

I have thought a lot about the father role in my life. I was a foster child, and our father visited us every Sunday, and was a truly kind and good man. But I had no role model for fatherhood. I loved the children but had no idea of what to do as a family man. Had I lived in the United States, perhaps I wouldn't have had as many options. But in Paris, we had a staff to help us care for the children, and Ann, coming from a family of eleven, knew exactly how to handle the situation.

I used to take the children to puppet shows in the park, to the zoo, to American softball games in the Bois de Boulogne. I also bought them expensive presents whenever I traveled away from home. I'm not too sure what my children made of me in those days, but as they grew older they accepted me as their father, and we are as close to each other now as we have ever been in our lives.

As time went on, the Parc Monceau became like a second home for the children, in spite of the rules. All children were permitted to play on the cement, but heaven help anyone who ran on the grass. Three uniformed gendarmes would blow their whistles at a child whose foot touched the green sod. Retrieving a ball or a wooden plane required permission from the *flics.*

To enforce their rules, the park police depended on an intricate informer system. If one child was caught removing sand from the sand pile, the arresting gendarme would let him go on condition that he report a serious crime, such as someone knocking down the tulips with a tricycle. The informer system was so successful that 99 percent of all crimes committed in the Parc Monceau were solved.

What drove me nuts was that the nannies were in constant competition to make sure their charges were the best dressed. Because our nurse Kay didn't want to lose face, she made Ann spend a king's ransom in clothes, more than it cost me to dress Ann.

Once I complained about all this, and Kay sniffed, "The Parc Monceau is not the Tuileries."

On one of my outings with the children, I took them to visit Audrey Hepburn, who was staying in Paris at the time. I often dropped in on visiting firemen booked at the fancy hotels to say hello, and very often the children came along. People appeared to welcome the visits. But not this time. Audrey Hepburn had become a friend, and one of the nicest people I knew. She was in Paris, making a movie, and as we passed her hotel, I said to the kids, "Let's go visit Audrey Hepburn." They didn't know who Audrey Hepburn was, but they were aware that whoever was in the hotel suite would immediately order up ice cream for them.

So it was with Audrey. After forty-five minutes, we all kissed each other goodbye. When I got home, I told Ann where we had been. She went white. "Do you know Audrey's pregnant?"

"So?"

"Connie just got over German measles. If Audrey gets the measles, she and the baby could have a terrible time."

I had no choice but to call Audrey and tell her about Connie. For six months, she had to undergo a series of gamma globulin shots.

In 1994, I watched Audrey's only son,

Sean, accept an award at the Oscars in the name of his mother. I thought to myself, "I hope he never finds out what I did to poor Audrey when she was carrying him."

At that time, all three of our children attended French schools; I took them in the morning, and Kay the nanny picked them up in the afternoon.

One time, Joel, then aged seven, and his best friend, Tiger, were waiting to be picked up. When Kay arrived, Tiger said to Joel, "Who's she?"

Joel replied, "She's my nurse."

"What does she do?" Tiger wanted to know.

"She cleans up my room, she makes my bed, and makes sure my clothes look good."

Tiger thought about this, then said, "I could use one of those."

I was shameless about using my children and their friends in my column. Here's one incident that I spun out for my readers. One day, Joel's friend Tiger called him and said, "My mother says I can't keep my cat, and if you don't take it, she is going to kill it, and it will be your fault."

"How can it be my fault if your mother

is going to kill it?" Joel asked.

Tiger said, "It will be your mother's fault because you won't take it."

When Joel told me this, I said, "I'm not going to take the cat."

Tiger called back in the evening, and said, "Are you going to take the cat?"

Joel said, "No, I can't. Why don't you give the cat to a café?"

"We tried that, but the cat jumped over the bar and broke the glasses, and scratched the bartender. They gave it back to us, because they said otherwise they were going to kill it."

"What about David Orshefsky? Give the cat to him."

"We tried to, but his dad said it was all right with him."

"To take the cat?"

"No, to kill it."

Tiger finally got rid of the cat by releasing it in the local food market. I saw Tiger the other day — forty years after the discussion — and he still blames me for not taking his cat.

At one point our family was featured on the CBS TV show *Person to Person.* Ed Murrow had originated the idea. The format was for the interviewer to go into your home and show the place as he talked to you.

Charlie Collingwood was the host in Paris, and one morning we found our apartment strewn with thousands of miles of cable and electronic equipment. We were supposed to be interviewed while eating lunch in our paneled dining room.

When Daniele the cook finally served the soufflé, the kids dove in and never bothered to look up. When people saw the show, they were really impressed by the children's decorum in front of the cameras. I never told them the secret. We hadn't fed the kids since breakfast, and if you starve your children they'll come through for you on TV every time.

All the Americans we knew in Paris had children and there were all sorts of celebrations. The most important one was the Easter egg hunt on Milt Orshefsky's lawn. Milt was the *Life* bureau chief. I dressed up as the Easter Bunny in a costume I had sent over from the United States. I continue to play this role at a friend's Easter party every year. The French, who take everything in stride, were completely thrown when they saw me in a taxi going down the avenue Foche in my bunny costume.

Since so many people knew about how we acquired the children, we became an information source for couples who wanted to adopt.

One was the wonderful actor Eddie Albert, and his wife, Margo. They were looking for a girl, so we directed them to the orphanage in Spain. Eddie went alone, and was well received by Mr. Mellado. He looked at several of the children, and then told Mellado, "We would like one that's having a hard time finding a home."

Mellado said, "I have a four-year-old who nobody wants, because she is too old."

Eddie asked to see the child. Maria strutted into the room with her hands on her hips. Eddie said, "How would you like to come home with me?" She responded in Spanish, "I shit in the bed."

Eddie hugged her, took her home to Margo, and they all lived happily ever after.

Chapter 5

Dukes, Counts, and *Flics*

Outside Paris, one of my favorite places was St. Moritz. I continued to be fascinated by the antics of the International Set, and finding myself in their company was always a heady experience. The lobby of the Palace Hotel in St. Moritz was a musical stage show. Everyone sipping hot chocolate had an aristocratic title.

Many afternoons I played chess in the lobby with a Spanish duke who kept the chess set, which was a family heirloom, in the hotel safe.

We became friends, and one day he said to me, "I have a problem. Whenever I get my bill, they charge me twenty Swiss francs for my dog."

"That's reasonable," I said. "After all, a dog can really muck up a room."

"Yes," he sighed, "but my dog has

been dead for nine years."

There was a French count who everyone knew was living off his American wife. One day, he showed me his Swiss watch. "Do you see this watch? I have it cleaned every time I come here and it doesn't lose three seconds a year."

I looked at him, and said, "What do you care?"

I think I spoiled his vacation.

Sometimes, the fun and games became serious. I was invited to a plush hunting club outside Kitzbühel, Austria, owned by a Polish count and his American wife. They took in paying guests and gave them a week of shooting and skiing in very luxurious surroundings. The club could accommodate twenty people at a time, not including the count and countess. Ann and I were guests. The first night, we were all seated at a table set with silver goblets and plates, candelabras, and exquisite flowers. Behind us were stationed butlers in Tyrolean uniforms. Everyone was quaffing wine and talking about the last bird they had killed.

Midway through the meal, a butler leaned over and whispered something to the count, who excused himself. He returned in about ten minutes, and announced, "You're not going to believe this. There was a man at the door and he asked if there were any free rooms — and he was a Jew!"

Everyone but Ann and me roared with laughter. I held on to the table with both hands. As soon as dinner was over, I called Eric Hawkins at the *Trib* and said, "Don't ask questions. Just send me a wire that General de Gaulle has granted me an interview on Wednesday." Ann and I got out of there the next morning, but it was a chilling experience I have never forgotten — mainly because the surroundings all seemed so civilized. At the same time, it was a stark reminder that attitudes had changed little in Europe since the war ended.

I must admit that while I found fun everywhere, I had emotional problems with West Germany. Every time I went there in the forties and fifties, I felt uncomfortable. I didn't know who the good Nazis were and who were the bad Nazis — and neither did anybody else.

I wrote a column about it which summed up these feelings.

I told about taking my son to a movie

titled *The Battle of the Coral Sea*, which showed the Japanese in World War II capturing and torturing Americans.

When we left the theater, my son said, "The Japanese were very bad people during the war, weren't they, Daddy?"

"Yes, but they are not bad people now — now they are good people."

"Why did they do bad things?"

"They didn't know they were doing bad things — they thought they were doing good things."

"Why didn't someone tell them they were doing bad things?" he asked.

"We tried to, but they wouldn't listen."

"Remember the war picture we saw some weeks ago, about the Germans beating up people in the concentration camps?"

"Yes."

"The Germans are bad people, aren't they?"

"No, they were bad people — but now they are good people."

"Are they different people?"

"No, they're the same people, at least many are the same people. You see, once you fight a war and you win, you can't stay mad at the people who started it — otherwise there would be another war."

"But in the movies they're bad people."

"Yes, that is to remind us they were bad people, but we're supposed to forget it."

He gave me a blank look, and said, "How many Russians did you kill during the war?"

"I didn't kill any Russians during the war. During the war, they were good people and they killed the bad Germans."

"Are there still bad Germans?"

"Of course. You see, the bad Germans want to kick all the good Germans out of Berlin."

"Why don't the Russians kill the bad Germans?"

"Because the Russians don't think their Germans are bad. They think they're good. And we believe their Germans are bad and our Germans are good. Now do you understand?"

Joel said, "No."

"Well," I said angrily, "it doesn't matter if you do or not — everyone else does."

People were always very nice to me in Germany which, for some reason, increased my sense of discomfort. Once, after I had moved to Washington, I traveled as a member of the press with Henry Kissinger, who was Secretary of State at the time. We were attending a spring festival in Frankfurt, and the adulation for Henry was unbelievable. He was completely surrounded, when a big fat man said to me, "If he had stayed in Germany, he would have been chancellor."

I blurted out, "Or a lampshade."

I wrote a series of columns on Hamburg, which featured the sleaziest vice section of any city in Europe. You could watch sexual performances of every sort in cabarets. If the same clubs had existed in Paris, I thought that they would have added a little extra spice to the town, but in Hamburg I felt depressed. The vice section also had women mud wrestlers, lesbian and homosexual bars, and dance halls where the ladies asked the men to dance. After my articles, the German Tourist Office canceled their advertising in the *Trib.*

If you don't count the Holocaust, my anti-German feelings were irrational. The hospitality was always wonderful, as was the food, the accommodations superb, and everything worked. But in those years after World War II, it was hard to blot out the horror they had inflicted on others.

But back to the parties. The one thing the rich could do well was give parties. I'm not talking about one of those black-tie events at the Waldorf-Astoria or an American country club. I'm talking about a Party.

I covered many of them for the paper — sometimes as an invited guest and others as a crasher. The most memorable was one given by Count Don Carlos de Bestegui in his palazzo in Venice in the early fifties. Bestegui was very rich, and decided to have a ball in which he asked guests to come in costumes befitting those of royal blood. This meant $5,000 wigs, gowns worth a small fortune, and of course all the jewelry that could be gathered up in Europe.

Women had hundreds of fittings in preparation. It was an evening that post-war Europe had never seen.

I wasn't invited.

That does not mean I was hurt. I didn't know Bestegui, and he certainly didn't know me. But something told me it was a big enough bash that I could somehow sneak in. I went to a theatrical store in Paris and rented a costume of Louis XIV. It was the last one in stock, and there were a few rips here and there, but I took it.

I flew to Venice just as excited as those who had invitations. When I arrived, I was informed by fellow newsmen that everyone had to come by gondola or motorboat up to the huge wooden front doors. Guards in eighteenth-century costume would be lined up along the palazzo dock to throw crashers into the canal. It wasn't going to be easy, but crashing parties of the International Set has never been easy.

My strategy was to arrive two hours before the guests, under the assumption that the guards wouldn't be checking those going in and out so early in the evening. I bought a large basket of flowers to deliver to the palazzo. In my Louis XIV costume, powdered wig and all, and with my basket on my lap, I rode down the canal, waving my white gloves to the crowd that was lined up along the way to cheer the rich and famous. They yelled, "Louis, Louis."

I acknowledged their enthusiasm by touching my hat as I had seen the Duke of Edinburgh do.

When I pulled up to the palazzo, hundreds of servants were scurrying in and out with champagne and provisions, and no one stopped me at the door.

I strode up to the first floor and found a comfortable bench in the hall, my flower basket still on my lap. An hour passed, when who should walk by but the count himself.

He stopped, and said, "Who are you?"

"I'm Louis the XIV," I replied.

He grabbed his guest list out of his pocket. "What is your name?"

"I don't have to tell you," I said.

"I'm calling the police." He ran downstairs and I ran upstairs. There were a dozen doors, and I ducked into the first one — which turned out to be a lavish bedroom, the size of the Excelsior Hotel lobby.

I checked out the palazzo balcony. This was much too public a place to hide, so I went back into the room and dived under the bed. I was not alone — two photographers from *Life* magazine were hiding there as well. One photographer, whom I knew, said, "Get the hell out of here."

"I can't. If they catch me, they'll catch you."

The other photographer said, "Merde."

The door opened, we heard footsteps, and right before my eyes were the most beautiful ankles I had ever seen in my life. They were two feet away from us. We heard a zipper, and then a dress dropped around her ankles. She stepped out of it. This was followed by a slip, which was followed by one silk stocking and then another. I bit my wrist to keep from crying out.

The ankles moved away and we heard the bath running. I looked out. Her costume was spread on the bed. When she came back from her bath, her towel dropped and the *Life* photographer hid his head in the rug.

It took an hour for her to dress. We stayed where we were until she finally got up and left the room. I was certain nothing at the party could top the show we had just witnessed.

The three of us crawled out from under the bed and headed out. By this time, there were enough arrivals that we could blend in with the crowd. I did the whole bit — ate lobster and caviar, drank champagne, and even danced with several Marie Antoinettes. This was a five-star party. I was so taken with it that when I left I personally thanked Don Carlos for it.

He said, "You honored me by coming."

I also attended a costume party in Biarritz held by the Marquis de Cuevas. I dressed as an American Indian and I had written on my chest "U.S. Go Home." It was a pretty good party, but I had been spoiled by Venice and a pair of anonymous ankles.

One more party story. Aly Khan gave one every spring at the Pré Catelan after the Grand Prix horse race. It was attended by the most beautiful women in Europe, and rumor had it that all of them had had something going with Aly at one time or another. I never found out if it was true or not. His father, the Aga Khan, told me that he had hired a tutor for Aly at an early age to teach the prince how to make love. One of the tricks the tutor taught him was to put a champagne bucket on either side of the bed, and place his hands in them to prolong the pleasure.

Aly always invited me to his party, and we passed the time guessing which of the women guests had benefited from the Aly Khan ice bucket routine.

Aly was a very nice man — a gentleman, charming and intelligent. At least, he was always nice to me, and therefore I never envied him his prodigious sporting life. When he died, a wag said, "If Aly had made love to all the women who claim they spent the last night with him, he would have been dead anyway."

Italy was a wonderful source of column material. One of the stories I covered there for *Collier's* magazine concerned the Italian sport of *pappagallismo.* The men who practiced it were known as the parrots of the street. They pursued women and yelled compliments at them, and also patted them on the behinds if they possibly could. They used what was known as the *mano morte,* or dead hand. The trick, of course, was to touch the person's behind without her knowing it. If the woman screamed, the man lost the game.

A friend of mine named Sue Graham told me that she was standing on a crowded bus once and she felt the man's hand behind her. She screamed, "Take your hands off me, you pig!" The man replied, "I wasn't pinching you. I was trying to steal your purse."

A former secretary, Jo Patrick, was

pinched on her bottom on a streetcar, and turned around angrily and slapped the man in the face, only to discover she had hit the wrong man.

With Italian grace, the slapped man said, "It wasn't me, but I wish it had been."

While the *mano morte* was considered crude by the women of Rome, they did not seem to mind the compliments that the parrots felt obligated to bestow on them. A proposal of marriage was not unheard of as a woman walked past a sidewalk café. Or a man might walk alongside a Roman beauty and cry, "God bless the mother who bore you," or "If I could be your chauffeur, I would drive you mad."

One lady named Jean (Giovanna) Salvadore told me she had been pursued by a man who told her he wished that he was a cobblestone so she would walk all over him. When she ignored him, he knelt on the sidewalk and said, "Tell me you have a sister who is only half as beautiful as you, and I will die happy, picturing her in my arms."

I once asked a parrot if he found pinching American women good sport.

"No," he said. "They are too thin."

Another time, I was in Rome, and I noticed an army of people collecting cigarette butts from the street. I asked one of them what he did with the butts, and he took me, for a fee, to the underground factory where they made new cigarettes out of the recycled tobacco. It was a large industry conducted in the basements of a poor section of the city. Italians were desperate for smokes, and the butts provided inexpensive cigarettes for the population. The butt collectors were masters at picking them from the sidewalks, and were paid according to how many they could sweep off the ground. Some had arrangements with café waiters, who emptied ashtrays for the butt-collectors' sacks.

Down the street was an even larger group of Italians who made counterfeit Parker and Schaefer pens and Rolex and Bulova watches, which looked exactly like the bona fide ones. They were works of art and sparkled better than the originals. The only way you could tell the difference between the counterfeit and the real ones was that a counterfeit watch stopped telling time two hours after you bought it. The Parker and Schaefer pens were another matter.

They were safe on the ground, but presented problems if you were flying. As soon as the plane reached 5,000 feet, all the ink in the pen started squirting out on a person's suit.

Of course, if you're talking about art, you have to talk about Paris. To enjoy the city, you must become an art junkie — not for the pictures of the Louvre necessarily, but for those being created by the artists of the time.

My favorite gallery, located on the Left Bank, was owned by a lady named Iris Clert, who specialized in instant masterpieces. Her painters produced pictures in record time.

"Many of my artists," she explained to me, "have become so depressed by the atom bomb that they have lost interest in immortality. To them, the act of painting has become more important than the finished work itself."

George Mathieu painted an entire show while riding a stationary bicycle. A Greek artist named Tsingos painted twenty pictures in an evening but only claimed two as masterpieces.

Yves Kline, one of the leaders of the instant school of art, daubed paint all over his model and then flung her down on the stretched-out canvas. The impressions left on the canvas after he picked her up became the paintings.

Many of Miss Clert's sculptors used junk to make their point. One filled fish bowls with electric razors and false teeth. Another approached the gallery with a cigar box. Inside was a white balloon. He said he had invented pneumatic sculpture.

"What makes it a work of art?" Iris asked.

The man replied, "My breath."

My all-time favorite artist in Paris was Jean Tinguely, a sculptor who invented a machine or machines that could produce abstract paintings. For a dollar, the viewer could create his or her own painting. He called his work "Immaterialization," which meant that he hung electric motors from the ceiling, which activated objects and sculptures at very high speeds so they became "immaterialized."

What made Mr. Tinguely the envy of Paris artists was that he could create a masterpiece in ten minutes. Tinguely told me that he had invented the ultimate anti-machine machine, because it never did the same thing twice. At the same time, it could copy anything a human could do without getting the artist's smock covered with paint. In one afternoon, it was possible for someone to create enough machine works of art to hold an exhibition.

Occasionally on a Saturday afternoon, I went over to the Left Bank to buy a piece of art. One day, I purchased a painting of a young man on a horse — a small oil which I fancied. I showed it to my friend Alain Bernheim.

"How much did you pay for it?" he asked.

"One hundred dollars."

"You dummy," he said. "They took you for a ride. I'll go with you the next time."

Several weeks later, I called him and asked him if he wanted to go looking for art. We went into a shop and I picked up a still life of apples.

"How much is it?" I asked the owner.

He told me in francs, which came to $200.

I turned to Alain, and said, "What do you think?"

He said, "The frame alone is worth it."

Even though I couldn't afford to buy an expensive painting, by luck I wound up with an original Picasso. This came about in a very unique way. I received quite a bit of mail when I was at the *Trib.* One day, a letter came from a young man in Philadelphia named Harvey Brodsky. His story was that he was in love with a girl named Gloria Segal. She had dumped him and Harvey wanted something dramatic to get her back. Harvey wrote that Gloria was Picasso's biggest fan, and he knew if he could get the artist's autograph, Gloria would be his forever.

It was a slow period in Paris, so I printed Harvey's letter as an example of how ridiculous my mail could get. The day the column appeared, David Duncan, the *Life* photographer, was in Venice with Picasso. David read the column to him, who, instead of laughing, was moved and took a colored pencil and drew a bouquet of flowers. At the top, he wrote "Pour Gloria Segal." Duncan had never seen Picasso do anything like that, and he called me in Paris and said excitedly, "I got it — I got a drawing for Gloria Segal."

I responded, "Frig Gloria Segal. What about me?"

David went back to Picasso and said that I had complained that I didn't get a drawing. Picasso looked at my picture in the newspaper, and did a drawing of the two of us having a drink together. He signed it "Pour Art Buchwald."

I have the picture, with the column on the back, in my study. In case you're wondering about what happened to Gloria and Harvey — nothing much. When the drawing was delivered to her by an A.P. reporter, all Gloria said was, "Harvey and I will always remain good friends."

Art was the reason that a friend of mine did time in a Paris jail. He was an artist himself, and shipped a large painting from London to Paris. He picked it up in the baggage department, but no one asked him for his claim check. So he told Air France they had lost his painting. The French get very upset when art is lost, so they immediately offered to compensate him for the painting, which he claimed was worth $1,000. Unfortunately, my friend was so proud of bilking the airline that he told everyone on the Left Bank. The police picked it up and raided my pal's room, where the painting was leaning against the wall. He spent three months in prison, and after he was released, they booted him out of the country in less than forty-eight hours. To the end, he maintained his sense of humor, and renamed the picture "Claim Check."

I had two run-ins with the police myself during my years in Paris. One concerned the Quat'z Bal, an artists' event of wild proportions. Artists and models stripped down to their barest, and then painted themselves all sorts of colors. The first part of the evening was devoted to running through the streets of the city, in and out of cafés and restaurants, and generally raising hell. The second part took place at the ball itself, where everyone danced, got drunk, and indulged in orgies.

I had arranged to go with a group of Beaux-Arts students. I wore a jock strap and was covered with silver paint. The evening started well, with ten young men and women dashing around, drinking wine, and making a lot of noise. Our big mistake was trying to crash Maxim's. We didn't get any further than the foyer, when we were surrounded by the police. They threw us all into a van, and we were taken to the police station at the Grand Palais on the Champs-Elysées and tossed into a cage across the room from the commandant's desk.

There, the students heckled the gendarmes. One of them shouted that I was a very important official of the Marshall Plan, and if I wasn't released immediately, all their bicycles would be taken away from them.

We assumed that we had been detained because we had crashed Maxim's, but the charge was not having proper identification papers. This is the biggest crime anyone can commit in France. So we gave our names and correct addresses, which were checked, and at three in the morning we were escorted to the ball in the same van that had picked us up earlier. The police assured us that there were no hard feelings.

It was an incredible evening, and one that I thought about for weeks after — not so much because of what I had experienced and witnessed but because I couldn't get the paint off my lower extremities.

Years later, I was in the Paris Hall of Records at the Cité, where Louis Jourdan and Claude Dauphin were making a TV movie about the Paris police. Jourdan was curious about the Jourdans who had committed crimes, and so was Dauphin. They looked up all the entries which had their last names to see what kind of criminal records they had. I looked up Buchwald, and found my own record when I had been arrested at the ball. I yelled to Dauphin, "I'm here." He called the head of the records, who looked at the card and said, "It's not serious. If it had been serious, we would have torn it up."

My only other run-in with the police took place on the evening of New Year's Day in 1959. Ann and I had thrown a very large and successful party on New Year's Eve, and the following evening we decided to eat the leftovers at the Bernheims' place. I took a tray and placed on it a silver bowl of chopped chicken liver, pickles, and rye bread. We called a taxi, but he turned out to be even crazier than the usual Parisian drivers. Ann got so upset, I ordered the driver to stop and let us out.

He said that he wouldn't until I paid him.

I told him that I wouldn't pay him until he let me out.

Ann was out of the cab on the sidewalk, when suddenly the driver put his foot on the gas pedal and took off into the night, with me in the backseat holding on to the tray. He drove up to a large police gate, and we were suddenly surrounded by six heavily armed gendarmes.

Lieutenant:	What the hell do you want here?
Taxi driver:	He won't pay me.
Lieutenant:	Do you know where you are?
Taxi driver:	The police station.
Lieutenant:	No, you idiot! It's a prison for Algerian terrorists. Now get out of here before we blow your brains out.

The driver was not about to give up. He drove to the Grand Palais police station — the same one in which I had been before. We both got out of the cab and I left my tray behind. We told our story to the sergeant. The taxi driver complained because I wouldn't pay him, and I complained because he would not let me take my chopped chicken liver out of his cab.

"What chicken liver?"

"I'm taking chopped chicken liver to my friends for the New Year," I explained.

This was too much for the sergeant, and he and his men went out to the taxi to see what chopped liver looked like. I invited each of them to taste it. They did, and then the sergeant said, "Pay the driver."

I paid the driver and took the tray and its contents out of the cab. Then I said to the sergeant, "Will you call me a taxi?"

To this day, people tell the story of a man holding a large silver tray with a bowl of chicken livers on it on New Year's Day in 1953, trying to hail a taxi with his head on the Champs-Elysées.

Since the *Trib* was located so near the Champs-Elysées, we had a ringside seat to the many demonstrations that were held there. Thousands of people would gather at the Arc de Triomphe and parade down to the Elysée palace. Some parades started at the place de la Concorde and ended at the place de la République.

An event that sent the French out into

the streets was the execution of the Rosenbergs. There were violent demonstrations throughout Paris, culminating with a confrontation in front of the American Embassy.

As an American, I had to explain to my French friends that I had nothing to do with the couple's electrocution, and I was against it, although I could not swear whether they were spies or not.

I'm not sure how acceptable my protest was, particularly when the Parisians did not want to hear from any Americans who were on their side — because it would spoil their demonstrations.

Not everyone came to Paris for pleasure. Many talented Americans were driven out by the McCarthy era because someone had labeled them Red. As a result, they were unable to find work in the United States, and very often these blacklisted writers ended up in Europe. Many of them worked with European film productions and wrote scripts under pseudonyms. Mostly, they were unable to get credit for their work, and producers took advantage of their precarious status and paid them poorly.

People suffered for years — sometimes all their lives — because of McCarthy. The majority of them were not Communists, but the very fact that someone had given their names to the House Un-American Activities Committee implied guilt. Larry Adler, the great harmonica player, was a victim, as was Paul Draper, the dancer, and Jules Dassin, the film director. Ben Barzman and Michael Wilson, and other fine screenwriters, were also blacklisted and so was African American novelist Richard Wright.

When Brown Reid came to the Paris *Herald Tribune* as publisher, he had a reputation as a Commie hunter. By the time he left the paper, he had mellowed, and, finally, as ambassador to Israel and then congressman, he became a very outspoken civil libertarian.

When the unions demonstrated on the streets, the Communists and Socialists refused to march together and were separated by a phalanx of police. My spot for demonstration-watching was Fouquet's. It was not only one of the best viewing places on the Champs-Elysées, but I could also enjoy my aperitif or a coffee while observing the action. Sometimes this didn't work out, such as the time some militant Communist truck drivers started throwing tables and chairs at the police, and the police retaliated by swinging their batons at the demonstrators. When this happened, I took my coffee and moved across the avenue to a less chic café, but one where the chairs weren't flying.

My greatest moment of protest-watching took place one afternoon when the Communist unions were protesting either French Fascism or a rise in the price of bread. To my amazement, leading the march, his arms locked with other left-wing celebrities, was Pablo Picasso.

The artist was smiling broadly, and he seemed very happy to be at the head of the parade. It was hard for me to reconcile this image of Picasso with his breathtaking artistic works — this short, stocky man, who appeared to get so much pleasure out of marching with the workers.

I joined in with the other spectators, chanting, "Picasso, Picasso, Picasso," clenching my fist in the air to show him I was on his side politically — which I wasn't. But I was an owner of one of his drawings, and I would do anything to sustain his popularity.

It was one of the highlights of my stay in Paris. To this day, when people ask me if I ever met Picasso, I always reply, "Met him? We used to hang out together on the Champs-Elysées all the time."

The French police were tough when they dealt with demonstrations. Once, my friend Bob Yoakum was on the Champs covering a riot, and a *flic* charged at him with a club. Yoakum whipped out his press card, and yelled, "Press, press." The policeman paused, checked Yoakum's credentials to make sure he was indeed "press," and then hit him over the head.

The funniest part of the demonstrations was that no matter what stage they were in, they had to end before midnight, because that is when the Métro stopped running. About eleven thirty, demonstrators and police would descend into the subway and ride home together, singing songs.

For an American, it was a circus we all accepted as part of living in Paris — and enjoyed because it had nothing to do with us.

In the early sixties, after de Gaulle

granted independence to Algeria, the situation got nastier and nastier. The Right and Left escalated their differences. The Right wing was made up of army veterans who had been forced to surrender in Indochina, and other colonials driven out of Algeria. They blamed the politicians in Paris, including de Gaulle, for their defeats. The Right was determined to hold on to Algeria no matter what the cost. Its members resorted to terrorism to make their point. One of its most unpleasant weapons was plastique, a substance used to blow up buildings and kill people. Plastique looked like Silly Putty, but with a simple time fuse the explosion was lethal.

We could be in bed at night and hear the bombs going off one or two blocks away. No one knew where they would explode next. Once, when we were making love, a bomb went off down the street. I said to Ann, "Did the earth move for you?" The lovemaking was over.

It wasn't all funny. I was dining at the Berkeley restaurant on a Sunday night, and I heard a loud explosion. It came from the vicinity of the Elysée Palace, so I rushed to see what had happened. It turned out that a plastique bomb had been placed in a trash container attached to a lamppost three feet off the ground, and when it exploded it had blown the legs off an English tourist.

The most dramatic moment came in 1961, when four French generals, Challe, Salan, Zeller, and Jouhaud, took over the town hall in Algiers and declared that Algeria would always remain French.

It was an act of treason and de Gaulle urged all Frenchmen to defy them. The problem was that de Gaulle had no army in France to protect his own country. The bulk of his troops were in Algeria, as well as in Germany. The French soldiers in Germany were under the command of a one-eyed war hero named General Massu. On Sunday night, a call was issued on TV for all Frenchmen to report to a regimental checkpoint and enlist in a citizen army to defend France.

Rumors had spread that the French Foreign Legion had left Algiers and was going to land in Paris. To stop the planes from landing, Paris buses were rolled out on the runways at Orly and

Le Bourget. I wrote a column a few days later about this aspect of the takeover, maintaining the French buses had performed the same service as the taxis had during the Battle of the Marne in World War I.

One of the enlistment centers for the citizen army was the Grand Palais, and I dashed down there to see what was going on. It was ten o'clock at night. The crowd gathered there was illuminated by weak searchlights, and I could see that most of the people who had shown up were veterans of World War II.

They were middle-class, middle-aged men who hadn't seen each other in twenty years. It was a reunion more than a call to arms. The men wrapped their arms around each other and hugged. They exchanged business cards. Few were in shape to fight, but they seemed willing to lay down their lives for France.

Although they were to constitute a citizen's army, the government refused to issue arms. The volunteers wound up instead with canteens and bayonets and World War II helmets. They had been urged by the prime minister to go to the airports, and talk the paratroopers into laying down their arms.

The turning point came when General Massu in Germany sided with de Gaulle, and brought his army back from Germany. But many say it was the transistor radio that won the battle against the insurrection. The draftees had them in the barracks in Algiers, and they heard de Gaulle's orders not to obey the generals, and they didn't.

While all this was going on, taxi drivers were offering to evacuate American tourists to Brussels for prices ranging from $500 to $1,000. Many Americans, unaware of the reality of the situation, decided to leave because if the cab prices were that high it had to mean conditions were unsafe.

Something weird but very French happened to me during this turbulent time. I received a call from an inspector in the Prefecture of Police, who said that he would like to come over right away. Ursula and I were scared. What did it mean — imprisonment, exile to Corsica, being drafted into the French army?

We cleaned up the office, set out a box of my most expensive cigars, and waited for the visitor, with trembling hands.

He arrived, nattily dressed in civilian clothes, with the everpresent briefcase in hand.

"Monsieur Buchwald, I am in charge of taking care of foreign VIPs in Paris, and I wish to know if there is anything the Paris police can do for you."

I looked at Ursula, and she looked at me. Then she said, "We are very happy, Monsieur l'Inspecteur. The police have always been good to us."

"Well," he said, handing us his card, "if you ever need anything — just call. That's why we're here."

He turned to leave, looking pleased to have accomplished his mission. His job was to massage the egos of foreign VIPs, and he damn well would not let a little thing like an attempted coup d'état interfere with his duty.

My friends in the press corps did not let anything going on in Paris interfere with our daily gin games. The setting for these games was the Time-Life offices overlooking the Place de la Concorde. The players were Frank White, Paris bureau chief of *Time* magazine; Milton Orshefsky, *Life* bureau chief; Stanley Karnow and photographers Dmitri Kessel and Gjon Mili.

On one occasion, I was playing with Frank White, when his secretary barged in and said that Ben Bradlee of *Newsweek* had been arrested. White, who was losing, said to her, "I told you not to disturb me when I am playing cards unless it is important." Then he turned to me with a big grin on his face, and said, "Gin."

During the same eventful period, Andy Heiskell, the Time-Life publisher, walked into Frank's office. I was concentrating on my hand and failed to say hello. Heiskell stalked out of the office and said to Frank's secretary, "Fire that man." She replied, "I can't — he doesn't work for us."

It was a time of great uncertainty in Paris. No one had any idea what would happen next. I attempted to find out what the various embassies were telling their nationals to do during the crisis.

First I called the U.S. Embassy, and was told, "Just sign the book in the lobby. If anything happens, we'll be in touch with you." That was consoling.

The British were more phlegmatic. When I claimed to be a worried British citizen, they said, "There is nothing going on to concern you. Go about your business as usual, and if anybody bothers you, just show them your passport and take the next train to Calais."

I finally called the Soviet Embassy — which was not easy. I asked a friend who spoke perfect Russian to say he was a Soviet citizen anxious about his safety and wanted to know what to do.

The man at the other end of the line said, "Report here immediately and bring your passport. Do not talk to anyone and be prepared to leave for Moscow."

I wrote that the only ones who really seemed to care about their people were the Russians.

The left-wing citizens weren't sure whose side the police were on, so many organized their own bodyguards. Philippe Grumbach, editor of the left-wing magazine *L'Express*, had a strategy for dealing with the right-wing disturbances in Paris. The magazine was the leader in exposing French army atrocities in Algeria.

When I went to visit Grumbach on the Champs-Elysées, I had to pass through a guard made up of heavyset gorillas in front of the building and in the reception room.

"Where did you get the wrestlers?" I asked him.

"They're French Jews who either were in concentration camps or are children of concentration-camp victims. When the war ended, they became physical fitness nuts and trained to be weight-lifters, wrestlers, and judo experts. They vowed that no one would ever do harm to them again. I heard about them and asked if they would like to be bodyguards for us, and they jumped at the chance. They said they didn't want to be paid. All they hope to get out of it is to break as many Fascist bones as possible."

All I could think about was that Polish count in Kitzbühel, and how interesting it would have been if a few of these guys had been along for the dinner that night.

Chapter 6

Stirring Up Trouble

Once upon a time, there lived in the Principalité of Monaco an American priest named Father J. Francis Tucker, who was Prince Rainier's confessor. He had been appointed to this post by the Vatican because of the battle between the French and Italians over the prince's soul and his real estate.

At this stage of his life, Rainier was a bachelor who loved fast cars, speedboats, and beautiful women — any one of which could get him killed. While he was entitled to his own lifestyle, a problem arose. If anything happened to the prince and he went to heaven without leaving an heir, Monaco would become part of France. Although the Principalité was no larger than Central Park, it had far more attractions, such as a palace, a zoo, fine hotels, and gambling casinos which attracted the richest people in the world. The French were dying to get their grubby hands on the place, and the Monegasques were frightened silly that something would happen to their prince before he produced an heir.

I know all this because Father Tucker told it to me when I interviewed him for a column. He laid it all on the line for publication. I suspect he did it to force the prince's hand and bring the young man to his senses.

The Father told me that his mission in life was to get the prince married.

"Do you have anyone in mind?" I asked him.

There was a twinkle in the priest's eye. "He seems to like Grace Kelly very much."

"Does he know Grace Kelly?" I asked.

"He met her once," came the reply. "When she was making *To Catch a Thief* with Cary Grant."

I wrote the story tongue-in-cheek, and titled it "If Grace Kelly Only Cared." The theme was that Grace, and Grace alone, had the ability to save Monaco.

Not long after the column appeared, I heard from a producer named Charles Feldman, who thought the idea of a prince and a movie actress set in Monaco would make a whale of a film. Charlie was rich and willing to pay me and another Hollywood writer named Cy Howard a goodly sum to do a script. We went to work on the picture, titled *Long Live Lilly,* and were 90 percent finished, when someone on the *Tribune* told me to look at the wires. I did, and what they were chattering was "Mr. and Mrs. Jack Kelly announced today the engagement of their daughter Grace to Prince Rainier of Monaco."

"Holy Mother of Monte Carlo," I screamed. "They stole our movie."

We called Charlie in the States, and he told us to keep going, as the story was better now than ever before — but our hearts weren't in it.

I blamed the whole thing on Father Tucker. Who else would take the trouble of destroying a person's film career?

Wounded and discouraged by this betrayal, I went down to Monaco, along with 1,400 other correspondents, to cover the wedding. There were more press than residents bivouacked on the tiny Principalité, and as with most wedding stories, if reporters didn't know anything, they made it up.

My companions on the Blue Train were Ben Bradlee, and Crosby Noyes from the *Washington Star.* While they knew all about the French government and Tito, I was the expert on Monaco. So they sucked up to me in hopes that I would give them enough fill-in to write the story. Bradlee said, "When we get there, we'll be like the Three Musketeers."

Noyes agreed: "One for all and all for one."

I raised my glass. "Friends until death."

We arrived at the railroad station in Monte Carlo and looked for a taxi. There weren't any. But two French reporters who had a tiny Renault shouted, "Ben, you want a ride to the hotel?" Ben and Crosby made a dash for it and climbed in the backseat. When I reached the car, Ben yelled, "There's no more room, Artie."

"What about the Three Musketeers?" I screamed, running alongside the car. Bradlee stuck his finger out the window.

So I was on my own. Crosby and Bradlee floundered writing their stories, because, being American Ivy Leaguers, they never did understand European royalty.

I will pause for a few moments to say a few words about Bradlee. Over the years, he has been one of my closest friends. I was best man at two of his weddings and I am godfather to Ben's son, Quinn. We first met when he was spokesman for Ambassador Douglas Dillon in 1952. As soon as I saw him, I said to myself, "White bread." This is my expression for WASPS — perhaps a little unfair, and I never say it out loud.

Ben was the perfect Renaissance man. He was handsome, he'd gone to all the right schools, his French was perfect, and he was a straight shooter. He also had humor, and we took an instant liking to one another. It was the beginning of a friendship that would span forty-five years. As the country would find out many years later, he also turned out to be one of the most out-standing newspaper editors of our time.

Back in Paris, he quit his job with Dillon to become bureau chief of *Newsweek* magazine, and moved into their offices on the fourth floor of the

Herald Tribune building, where we spent long afternoons playing gin rummy and shooting the bull. Bradlee will deny this, but one of the reasons I like him so much is that he always held picture cards at the end of a gin hand for no apparent reason.

In spite of his card-playing, I respected him. He went back to the U.S., first as Washington bureau chief for *Newsweek*, and then as editor of the *Washington Post*. Bradlee was a great editor because he was able to make his reporters do far more than they thought they could when covering a story — whether it was Watergate or Mayor Marion Barry's circus. He had very high standards and was able to impart them to the staff. He also was so self-assured that he didn't have to prove to anyone who he was.

Ben and I have shared many memorable moments together — the worst was when President Kennedy was shot. I ran to his office in the National Press building, and Ben was there alone, staring at the TV. His face was ashen. "Hang on, buddy, hang on," he was yelling at the screen. When they announced that Kennedy was dead, Ben and I threw our arms around one another and cried.

Bradlee is a good man, and despite what he did to me in Monaco, I have always believed that he wishes me well.

I decided to go for broke on the column I filed for the *Trib*. In my piece, I warned the reader not to expect me to be invited to the wedding ceremonies, because the Grimaldis and the Buchwalds had been feuding for five hundred years. I said it had started with the first Grimaldi and the first Buchwald, who was an AP stringer. I reported that my ancestor had claimed that Grimaldi, who played lawn tennis, constantly foot-faulted. If anyone dared to point this out to Grimaldi, however, he ordered his head chopped off and hung in the tennis club's bar.

I traced the feud all the way down to present times, when my aunt Molly had refused to invite Rainier to my cousin Joseph's wedding in Brooklyn. Because of Aunt Molly's hostility, Rainier was getting even by not inviting me to his.

The story appeared in the next morning's *Tribune* — and that afternoon an invitation to the wedding was hand-delivered to me from the palace.

I borrowed a set of white tie and tails from the waiter at the Hôtel de Paris. It didn't fit, but it didn't stop me from becoming one of the chosen few to sit in the cathedral and also to eat a piece of wedding cake in the palace court-yard. My good luck was not appreciated by my colleagues, who by this time I considered to be disgusting gossip-mongers.

I didn't see too much of the wedding ceremony itself because King Farouk was seated in front of me, and when he stood, which he did for most of the ceremony, I was staring at one of the most unattractive derrières in the world. I have to confess I never did care for King Farouk. He was greedy and unattractive and gave all ruling mon-archs of that time a bad name. Here's an example of what I mean about his indifference to the plight of his people. I was in the lobby of the Hôtel Royal in Deauville, and the press agent Guido Orlando — you remember, the guy who tried to get in to see de Gaulle in 1948 — went up to Farouk's secretary and said, "His Majesty is in deep doodoo. He's getting bad press around the world because he is gambling so much money away. Why don't we hold a press conference to say that the only reason the king gambles is to help the widows and orphans of Egypt?"

The secretary said he would take it up with Farouk. He came down the next morning, and said, "His Majesty says what he wins, he keeps."

Despite having to look at a royal backside throughout the wedding, I had a great time. I mingled with European royalty, not as a grubby newspaperman but as an invited guest. I recall remarking to a baron about the press in the street, "When *will* they leave us alone?" There were toasts and the cutting of the wedding cake. I felt so good that the Grimaldis had made up with the Buchwalds. I even told Jack Kelly that some day I hoped my daughter would marry Princess Grace's son.

After the wedding, I rushed to a phone to call Ann in Paris. I gave her a full report — the clothes, the wedding ceremony, the guest list, the cake. I paused for a moment and I sensed a cold chill from Paris. "What's wrong?" I asked.

Ann said, "It's my birthday."

"Wait," I said, "I was coming to that."

I often marvel at how varied my job

on the *Trib* was. Because the column was being widely read, I was encouraged by my editors to cover all kinds of important events. I attended Queen Elizabeth's coronation, shivering in the rain on a muddy slope in Hyde Park. I went to Ascot and managed to get into the royal enclosure, in a suit rented from Moss Bros. and insured by Lloyd's of London for a premium of $1. The policy, written by an English friend, David Metcalfe, who was a member of a Lloyd's of London syndicate, stated that the suit was only covered if anything happened to it while I was in the presence of the Queen or a member of the royal family. It was one of those high-risk policies, but David wanted to prove that Lloyd's would gamble on anything.

I was also a guest on a British weekend in the country for a bat hunt. The event was held at Old Surrey Hall in Sussex, the home of Lt. Colonel Ian Anderson. It was rare for an American to be invited to attend a British bat hunt, so I felt tremendously honored when I got the call from Mrs. Anderson, whom I had met at a garden party for the Duchess of Kent. I had no idea what to wear to a bat hunt, since most of the action takes place between midnight and three in the morning. Anderson supplied me with the uniform, which turned out to be a hair net, a bathrobe, and sneakers.

The weather was perfect for the occasion. It was raining, there was thunder and lightning, and the wind whistled through the house.

The colonel handed me a warped tennis racket. "This is your weapon. Take a few practice swings."

Among the guests was Dr. Robin Beare, an eminent plastic surgeon. He had been asked to accompany the hunt in case anyone got hurt.

Once inside the great hall, we were all assigned positions. Since I was new to the pursuit, I was told I could stand on a couch. The lights were dimmed, and the bats flew down at incredible speed. Everyone started to swing at once, but no one came near a hit. I couldn't help noticing the different styles people had adopted to swing at the bats. One guest did the chop, another the forehand defense swing. It didn't seem to matter — the bats had our number. After every fly-by, we drank another round of scotch and tried for a kill. Only towards the end of the evening did Colonel Anderson strike a bat's wing by accident. When he moved in for the big swing, the bat flew to the top of the house, and the score read: Five quarts of scotch, no bats at all. Over the years, when someone would start discussing fox-hunting in Britain, I'd say, with great smugness, "It's nothing compared to hunting bats in your bathrobe."

I went punting on the Thames at Henley, and beagling on the moors of Scotland, and coursing with dogs in Ireland. And I was invited to go shooting on the estate of a lord whose name wouldn't mean anything to you. This event involved being "fitted" for a shot-gun at Purdy's in London.

Pheasant-hunting was new to me, and something I had never learned at the Hebrew Orphan Asylum. Each of us was given a position in a ditch. A beater in the bushes made the pheasants fly, at which time we shot at them. Behind each guest was a loader, who also had a shotgun. When things weren't going well, he shot at the same time I did, and if anything fell out of the sky, he would say, "Good shot, sir." Everyone down the line commented on my shooting, and I walked back to the mansion with a brace of pheasants, which in my heart of hearts, I knew had been struck down by my loader.

Once I went fox-hunting with John Huston in Ireland. I didn't ride with the hounds but followed closely in a jeep. The following day, I wrote a piece suggesting that the best way to improve the sport was to lay poison on the ground, which the fox would eat. This would save all the trouble of having to get up in a fancy outfit and ride after him.

Huston, who was Master of the Hounds in County Kildare, was chewed out by his flock for having invited such an offensive person to his home.

While I did not support the fox hunters, I did write a favorable article about the high tea served after the hunt. I gave the meal served around four o'clock top marks, and commented, "If you don't enjoy seeing a fox chased across the meadows and driven into a hole by the dogs, I recommend the scrambled eggs, scones, and strawberry jam served after the hunt is over."

John Huston was one of the most interesting people I met in Europe. He could be cruel and funny at the same time. He was not only a master of hounds, he was a genius.

When John directed *Moby-Dick*, I went to Youghal in Ireland to report on the production. Youghal is a small seaside town, and John transformed it into New Bedford, Massachusetts, because it looked more like New England than New England.

The buildings were modified to suit the film, but the people were changed forever. There was a need for cooperation between the town and the production company, so John hired the local incumbent politicians to organize the work. The mayor became the contractor, while another politician owned all the boats used in the movie. The plum job went to the person who rounded up extras. This gentleman followed the customs of the area. He gave the upper-class people the best costumes and the working-class candidates the tattered peasant clothes. As soon as they were in costume, the groups split just as they did in real life, to the extent that the upper classes refused to eat with their less fortunate counterparts.

There was one pub where we all hung

out, mainly because one of the local production assistant's brothers owned it. The bar was jammed with horse fanciers. All they talked about was horses, until John Huston and Gregory Peck — Captain Ahab in the film — walked in. Then the patrons broke into song with "Did Your Mother Come From Ireland" or "My Wild Irish Rose." John recognized the scam from the start and ate it up.

The day before shooting began, I noticed a man with a wooden leg standing at the bar. His name was Paddy Ryan, and he was being treated as a hero by the townspeople. Word had gotten out that Gregory Peck would need a stand-in for the Captain Ahab long-shots, and Paddy was the only one in the county with a wooden leg.

"Does he have the job?" I asked.

"No. He's going over the casting in a few minutes," came the reply.

It sounded like a good story, so I accompanied Paddy over to the casting office. He said cockily, "I hear you need someone with a wooden leg."

The casting director leaned over the table and said, "Wrong leg."

I loved going to Britain. It was another

world compared to the Continent. Whenever I think of England, I recall a story told by a country gentleman. He was on his way to a stately home. The weather was freezing, the roads were icy, and he was close to acquiring frostbite.

When he arrived at the door, it was opened by the butler. "God, Blagdon, it's freezing out here." Blagdon bowed and replied, "Wait until you get inside, sir."

Another memorable British weekend for me was when I was invited to the Duke of Bedford's stately home, Woburn Abbey, for the weekend. The duke was the first to convert his private home into a paid attraction. He had been forced to do this to pay the enormous taxes owed to the government on the death of his father. He'd opened a souvenir shop and imposed an admission charge to take the tour of the house and grounds. At first, the other dukes scorned what Bedford had done, but pretty soon they were all doing the same thing.

A guest of the Bedfords was expected to work. We were each assigned a location to act as guards and guides. My spot was on the second floor, overlooking a long hall filled with enormous portraits of generations of dukes and duchesses from the past.

Visitors were curious to know which was which, and to hear some interesting fact about each of them. At first when I was asked, I claimed ignorance, but then, when I saw the disappointment on people's faces, I gave responses.

It went like this: "Who is the chap up there?"

"That's the first Duke of Bedford. He killed his wife to marry the second duchess, and he in turn was killed by her son. We're lucky to have a portrait of him."

"The beautiful lady in the white wig. Where does she fit in?"

"She was the mother of the fifth Duke of Bedford, who tried to stop her son from marrying Catherine of Barcelona, because it was rumored Catherine could have no orgasms."

As the day wore on, I became more imaginative in my stories, even giving one of the duke's ancestors a painful venereal disease he picked up while serving with the Royal Hussars in Turkey.

That evening, as we counted the receipts of the day in the dining room, I told the duke what I had been saying about his family.

"Good show," he said, slapping me on the back. "We should have thought of that sooner."

Not every one of my visits was associated with glamorous places. I once covered a chess championship in Manchester, which is not Florence and probably should be missed by the tourists. The city did not impress me.

The actress Tallulah Bankhead was a pal, very funny and very sexy. She told me a story of being in Manchester one weekend, where she met Randolph Churchill. They spent the time in bed together, with the occasional breaks for room service. Randolph was smitten, and when he got back to London, he kept calling Tallulah at her room in the Dorchester Hotel. She refused to take his calls. Finally, Randolph sent her two dozen red roses, with an attached note, "How could you treat me like this after what happened in Manchester?"

Tallulah wrote on the other side, "Randolph, it wasn't you — it was Manchester."

It was in England that I got my best scam story. It took place at Cartier's on Bond Street in London. A well-dressed man came in and admired a necklace in the window that was priced at 150,000 pounds. He came in every day to look at it. As the weeks went by, the salespeople became used to his daily visits. Finally, on a Saturday morning, he said he'd take it. Would they accept a check? The salesperson nervously called his superior at home and asked for instructions. The superior told him to check with Claridge's Hotel, where the client was staying. Claridge's reported that the man had a large suite and seemed to be well off. So the decision was made to sell him the necklace.

An hour later, a man saying he was a pawnbroker called, and said that a well-dressed man had come in and offered to sell him a new Cartier's necklace for 20,000 pounds. The pawnbroker knew the piece was worth a lot more than that, and thought Cartier's should be alerted. All the alarm bells in Cartier's went off.

"Did he say where he was going?"

"He mentioned taking the ferry at Dover."

Cartier's called the police and asked them to pick up their customer, which they did. They found the necklace on him and he was thrown in jail for the weekend.

Now this is the part of the story I like the best. On Monday morning, the man's check proved to be good and cleared his bank. He sued for false arrest, and Cartier's had to settle for *twice* what the necklace was worth.

It was an inspired tale, and if anyone tries to steal the idea for a movie, I will sue him.

I continued to be fascinated by the interaction of the different European nationalities and their behavior toward Americans. When I traveled from country to country, I always took note of how local inhabitants conducted business.

For example, if I went into a Paris haberdashery to buy a shirt, the salesman would immediately tell me he didn't have one in my size — before I asked. When I'd informed him I was prepared to take another size, he would become upset and start talking to someone else at the counter. If he didn't make a sale, he considered that a good day.

The British were something else. In London their shirt salesmen would sneer at me. If I asked for a button-down collar, they would shake their heads in disgust. Stripes, as everyone knows, were last year's style, and only Americans would want pockets on their shirts, etc. They were willing to sell me one or even make one for an American customer, but they behaved as if it was such a waste.

The Italian shirtmaker, on the other hand, treated me like a long-lost brother the moment I walked in the door. He wanted to know where I was from and whether I knew his cousin Tony in Hackensack, or his sister Angela, who was married to an Irish cop named Pat in Boston. Before he took my measurements, he presented me with a cup of steaming espresso. No matter what kind of shirt I wanted, he assured me that I was a man of fashion. Without asking, he would break into a Verdi aria while writing down my measurements. In gratitude, I would purchase six shirts instead of one.

The French had a reputation for personal rudeness in stores — at least as far as many Americans were concerned — but the one incident of rudeness I remember vividly took place in London, not Paris. I was in Simpson's, the Piccadilly department store, purchasing a pair of Daks. The fly had buttons, as did most English pants. "Could I have a zipper instead of a button fly?" I asked. "Of course, sir," the salesman said, with an oily grin. He took the pants and returned to the counter, not realizing that I was walking behind him. Then he said to a fellow salesman, "Silly bugger wants a zipper on his fly."

I only had one row with a British politician during my years in Europe. I was dining at a private home in London, and Hugh Gaitskell, the leader of the Labour Party, was there. He started a tirade about Prime Minister Harold Macmillan which never seemed to end. I asked him if he would grant me an interview, and he said that he would, provided I forgot what he had said at dinner.

Next day in the dining room of the House of Commons, he told me even worse things about Macmillan, which I wrote down. Then he called me the following day and asked me to forget what he had said on Monday. I asked him what he really wanted to say, and he told me even worse things than before.

My article appeared and was greeted with a yawn on the Continent, but it was hot stuff for the British papers, which put the interview on the front page. Gaitskell was outraged, and said that he had never spoken to me for attribution. His lawyer wrote to the *Herald Tribune* lawyer, threatening action, but since Gaitskell had said terrible things about Macmillan almost every day, our lawyers were not worried.

One day, while walking down Piccadilly, I thought of an idea for a provocative column. I decided to place an advertisement on the front page of the *Times* of London which said, "Would like to hear from people who dislike Americans and their reasons why."

The response was more than I had expected. Before the storm died down, I had received over three hundred letters, and a mixed bag it was. Many truly did dislike Americans, and for the usual reasons — brash, patronizing, refusal to speak good English. But there were others harboring grudges of long, long ago.

An English gentleman said he had been in a bar in Bombay in 1923, and these drunken American sailors had come in and torn the place apart. They were, he said, nothing but savages, and he has distrusted Americans ever since.

World War II had left its wounds, and some of the mail concerned Americans stealing English women, or, worse still, buying up all the good English Wedgwood with American dollars.

But some of the mail was anti-me. The writers, English admirers of America, assumed I was British, and so they attacked me for stirring up trouble with a good ally. These letters were pro-American and I turned them over to the U.S. Embassy as a patriotic duty.

I was also pleased with the letter from the editor of the *Daily Express* who urged me to contact him as soon as possible, because he thought the responses might make a good newspaper article.

Which brings me to the subject of anti-Americanism in Europe in the forties and fifties. It may have existed, but it was never on a personal level. There had to be hurt feelings while Europeans were just getting on their feet and some Americans lorded it all over them — trying to trade chocolate bars and Kleenex for things of value. The language barrier in Europe always caused misunderstanding, particularly between American citizens and French taxi cab drivers. Continuing jokes about France's toilet paper didn't help, either.

What saved me was that early in my residency I discovered that the French did not like each other. If this was true, why should they like us? To be negative was part of their culture. They were prepared to take a contrary position on any subject or issue. My best example was when my hot-water heater broke. I called the plumber, who arrived prepared to tell me it couldn't be fixed. I was waiting for him, and when he said from his ladder, "It is impossible to fix this hot water heater. This valve they do not make anymore, this pipe is broken," I chimed in, "Of course it is impossible to fix. No one could fix that hot-water heater."

His face reddened, and he stared me straight in the eyes and said, "I could fix that hot-water heater."

I scoffed. "I doubt it." My wife yelled, "For God's sake, let him try."

One of the most anti-American people I ever met was the English writer Nancy Mitford. I once asked her what American she disliked the most. She replied, "Abraham Lincoln. I detest Abraham Lincoln. When I read the book *The Day Lincoln Was Shot*, I was so afraid that he would go to the wrong theater. What was the name of that beautiful man who shot him — John Wilkes Booth? Yes, I like him very much."

It was a historical first. I didn't know anyone who was prepared to go on record with a kind word for Lincoln's assassin.

While the ugly American probably had his greatest moments in the 1950s and 1960s, the British tourist was in a class of his own. Disdainful and suspicious of people who drove on the wrong side of the road, the British tourists were mocked by the French even more than the Americans.

My expert on this subject was the actor Robert Morley.

He and I were sitting in a café in Cannes, and he told me, "The British tourist is always happy abroad as long as the natives are waiters. But if the natives start bathing in the same sea with us, we feel that there's something wrong. We have always believed the French are only useful if they stand two paces behind our chair while holding a bottle of wine."

I asked him if he thought that the British tourist was out of touch with the Riviera.

"Just yesterday, an English chap said to me in the Carlton lobby, 'You'll feel a little out of it here. They don't get the dog racing results from Birmingham, only from London.' "

Probably one of my favorite British people of all time was Somerset Maugham. He had been a household name in my youth and I was thrilled to get to know him in Europe. He became a friend and I was very happy about that. He invited me for lunch one day at his beautiful home on Cap Ferrat. I admired a wooden panel with a Gauguin painting on it and asked him how he had acquired it.

He said, "There's an interesting story behind that. I went to Tahiti years ago and asked to see where Gauguin had lived. They took me to this very simple house, which was occupied at the time by a local family. Once inside, I looked at the door and realized it was one of his paintings. I told the occupant that I would love to buy the door. He told me that I couldn't have it. I asked him why not. He said, 'Where would I get another door?' So I found a workman in town to make a new door for him, and I bought this one."

Maugham was a real gentleman. Once I wrote a column stating that there were so many yachts and villas on the Riviera that there was a shortage of guests, and that I had once gone down to the Monte Carlo port to board someone's boat and yelled, "Sam, send me a boat," and every yacht in the harbor had lowered one. I also wrote that the situation was so bad that a journalist staying with Lady Kenmare was the rudest person in the world, but they couldn't ask him to leave because they needed a fourth for bridge. When the article appeared, the journalist, the late Godfrey Winn, instructed his solicitor to send me a letter saying that he would take action, as he was the only newsperson staying with Lady Kenmare at that time.

I called Maugham up and said, "Did you know that son of a bitch Godfrey is going to sue me, because I wrote a satirical piece about the Riviera?"

Maugham was incensed, and said with his stammer, "Th-tha-at's ri-dic-ulous, I'll c-all you b-aack."

He did and said, "Dd-on't wor-ry, hh-e's nn-o-t go-ing tt-o sue yy-ou."

"What did you tell him?" I asked.

"I said, 'Go-odf-rrey, i-f you s-ue Bb-uuchwald, y-ou can n-ev-er cc-ome to m-y h-ouse for din-ner a-gain.' "

David Niven, the actor, was another charming Englishman. Like Maugham, he also had a home on Cap Ferrat. French law forbade people getting on his beach by foot but permitted them to stay there if they arrived by sea. As soon as they knew whose house it was, people swam over from other places and lay on the rocks just off his beach. Niven, who was the mildest of men, went berserk every time he saw someone on his rocks, eating their food and waving to him. I was with him many times when he started to scream, "Get off my rocks." People just smiled back.

Just the idea of anyone being on his rocks drove Niven around the bend. We would be at the Monte Carlo casino, and suddenly he would turn to me and say, "I know they're on my rocks."

"David, it's midnight. Why do you care who's on your rocks at this hour?"

He replied, "Only someone who didn't own a beach would ask such a dumb question."

I was always settling personal scores in the column. I decided one day that I would personally silence the bells of the American Cathedral. The bells had been a gift from Holland, and the minister was so pleased with them he played them on the hour. I lived across the street from the cathedral, and the sound was driving me batty, so I wrote a letter to the *Herald Tribune* as if from a French housewife. It said, "My husband works on the Métro all night long, and he can't sleep in the daytime because the Americans insist on ringing their church bells. Don't the people at your church have any respect for the French worker?"

The letter started a flood of mail over whether the Americans should or should not ring their bells. I added a few more. The publisher of the Paris *Herald Tribune* at that time was also on the board of the cathedral, and he was catching hell about the flap. He knew I had something to do with the letters but wasn't quite sure what it was. So he called me in and said, "Don't we have any letters in favor of the bells?"

"Of course, sir," I said. I went back into the city room and said, "Weare wants a letter for the bells." I sat down and wrote what turned out to be the final note on the subject. It read, "I don't know what all the fuss is about the bells. I've never heard them." The letter was signed, "Angelo Baltirini, Rome, Italy."

My columns got me in trouble sometimes. As a movie critic for the *Trib,* I once wrote an unfavorable review of *Joan of Arc,* which had had its premier at the Paris Opera House.

Walter Wanger, the producer, was furious when he read it, and at an American Club luncheon he said I was immature and had an inferiority complex, and that was why I could not give his picture a good review. He had a point. But after the lunch, when reporters came up to me and asked me what I had to say, I said, "In France, when a producer doesn't like what a critic says, he challenges him to a duel. If Mr. Wanger will send his seconds, we will discuss weapons."

The story hit the wire service and made headlines in the French newspapers. *France Soir*'s front page read "Two Americans to Fight for the Virgin of Orleans."

I became famous for fifteen minutes. Ann was very disturbed about the publicity and, instead of enjoying it, was embarrassed. For years, we argued about whether it had been a smart move.

Whenever we had a good fight, she would say, "You haven't changed since that dumb thing you did with Walter Wanger."

The same situation almost arose with the actor Rex Harrison. He was bowing out of the London production of *My Fair Lady*, and I interviewed him about his feelings on the show. He told me for attribution that he didn't think anyone could play Professor Higgins as well as he could, and he also had some unkind words about his leading ladies.

Nothing happened when the article appeared, but the following day, the

British papers picked it up and started to bash Harrison no end. He blamed me for quoting him, although he didn't deny the accuracy of what I wrote.

As luck would have it, I was dining at a small French restaurant called Fabien when Harrison came in with his wife, Kay Kendall, and the director Stanley Donen. I was with six other people. Kay came over to our table and started slapping my face. All I could do was duck and yell at Harrison to get her away from me.

Ann wanted to slug Kay and I felt like slugging Donen.

Finally, Rex said, "Come outside and we'll settle this once and for all."

I replied, "I'm eating dinner. I'll meet you tomorrow in the Bois de Boulogne."

"Tomorrow in the Bois," Harrison said, holding up his fist like John L. Sullivan.

The next morning, I called Harrison to make sure he would show up. He said he had no intention of providing me with another column.

The article that really catapulted me to fame took place when President Dwight Eisenhower came to Paris in 1957 for a NATO conference. He carried

the usual baggage of White House correspondents — many of whom were
content to eat out of Press Secretary
James Hagerty's hand.

Press headquarters was the Crillon
Hotel. I attended a presidential press
briefing and was amazed how well it
was going. Eisenhower had been sick,
so most of the questions were about his
health.

There was nothing of substance discussed at the briefing, but I understood
that that was the agreement Hagerty
had with the White House reporters.
"Don't ask me any hard questions, and
I'll see that you don't get any hard
answers. That way you can get to see
the Folies-Bergère tonight."

I decided to write a spoof of a Hagerty
press briefing. I claimed it took place at
midnight, because Hagerty was delayed
at the Lido Cabaret (Hagerty had a
reputation for enjoying night life).

This is how it went:

Q. Jim, whose idea was it for the
   president to go to sleep?
A. It was the president's idea.
Q. What did he say to the secretary
   of state?

A. He said, "Good night, Foster."

Q. Do you have any idea what the president is dreaming right now?

A. No, the president has never revealed to me any of his dreams.

Q. When the president went to sleep, how many blankets were on his bed?

A. Maybe two or three. But certainly no more than he uses in Washington.

Q. Jim, could one have been kicked off during the night?

A. Yes, that could be possible but it's highly unlikely.

The *Tribune* put the column on the front page — a rare occurrence — and Hagerty hit the fan. He called a special NATO press briefing the next morning to deny the spoof. He accused me of writing "unadulterated rot." The reporters, pencils poised to get my response, quoted me as saying, "Hagerty is wrong — I write adulterated rot."

Everybody filed their stories, and as they say in the Mafia, I was a made man. The great oracle Arthur Krock defended me, as did columnist Doris Fleeson. I was the subject of favorable editorials around the world. To make matters worse for Hagerty, Eisenhower told him to simmer down.

It was a glorious, unexpected moment of fame and gave me notoriety beyond my wildest dreams. In many ways, the feeling was no different than when I was grandstanding in show-and-tell at Public School 35.

I want the record to show that I didn't pick on Jim Hagerty to get famous. But in the humor business your targets have to be those on top of the heap — and a president's press secretary is as near the top as you can get.

The years have gone by, but to this day I owe a lot to James Hagerty. We made up long after he left the White House, and when we saw each other in the late years, we had a good time together. I always gave him a big hug. I owed him a lot and I wanted him to know that I hadn't forgotten it.

I had a misunderstanding with Lyndon Johnson when he was vice president. He was visiting Paris, and David Schoenbrun, the CBS correspondent, called me at two in the afternoon and said, "How would you like to have dinner with the vice president of the United

States?" I replied that I thought that would be very nice. "Meet us at Maxim's at eight thirty P.M." I called Ann and said, "Guess what? We're going to have dinner with the vice president and Mrs. Johnson at Maxim's." Ann giggled and said, "I was thawing hamburgers for tonight."

Then she cried, "I have to go to the hairdresser and have my nails done, and then get my dress out of the cleaners."

"Don't worry," I told her. "It will be worth it."

An hour later, Schoenbrun called again. "They don't want you."

"What the hell do you mean, they don't want me?"

"They don't trust you."

"Why didn't you ask them before you asked me?"

"It never entered my mind that Johnson had even heard of you."

I had two problems. One was to get Ann and call her off from spending fifty dollars at the hairdresser. The other was that I had to write a column. Since the deadline was upon me, I had the perfect subject: How I almost had dinner with the vice president of the United

States. The column was easy — calming Ann down took more work. She was in tears when I told her that the Johnsons didn't want us. To make it up to her, I promised to take her to Lasserre for dinner.

After the column appeared, I received a hand-written note from Johnson, saying, "Sorry we missed in Paris — the next time Lady Bird and I are there, we'll have hamburgers with you and Mrs. Buchwald."

Chapter 7

To Cairo, and Beyond

I found myself on the road more and more. Ann told all our friends that at first she was pleased with my professional gallivanting, but soon the glamour wore off and she was sorry she hadn't married a rich French waiter. To make matters worse, a few of her "friends" kept saying to her, "Aren't you afraid Art will wind up with another woman in Estonia?"

I never did horse around, mainly because it would interfere with my search for column ideas, and also since my picture appeared with the column, I would be recognized immediately if I was seen romping in the ruins of Pompeii with Jane Russell or Sophia Loren.

Once I told Ann, "Someday I'm going to be in some god-forsaken place and I won't be able to get through on the telephone. So I'm going to take out the local town harlot, and you'll hear about it in twenty minutes, and you will know that I am safe."

Paris lends itself to falling in and out of love. Although I didn't have any affairs, my American friends did. Some adopted the French habit of having one without breaking up their marriages. One of Paris's great customs was to meet one's paramour between the hours of "cinq à sept" in the afternoon. This was the time the French set aside for aperitifs, love, and bicycling before going home to dinner. When I first came to Paris, paying a visit to a mistress was not a big problem. But as more and more traffic appeared on the streets, it became so bad that sometimes a couple only had fifteen minutes to shower and get in and out of bed. I do not know this from experience, but it was related to me by friends, all of whom had bags under their eyes.

Paris hotels and restaurants made life a great deal easier for lovers. There were small hotels serving delicious food downstairs, and beautifully furnished three-star lovers' quarters upstairs.

When checking into a respectable

auberge in the country, the fact that the person's identity papers did not match the registration signatures on the books was overlooked by the police.

The most famous of all restaurants to cater to romantics was the Restaurant Lapérouse, located on the quai des Grands-Augustins. It had private dining rooms, decorated in heavy red velvet with soft cushions. The waiters were trained never to enter the rooms unless they were alerted by a buzzer.

The restaurant was a three-star establishment and was patronized by politicians, wealthy French businessmen, and beautiful people from around the world. If the walls could talk, I am sure someone could get a 6,000,000-franc book advance.

Some houses of ill repute were even protected by the French government. It was common knowledge that a famous madame worked for two masters — the rich customers and the French secret service, who bugged all the rooms. The French foreign office had diplomats and foreigners of high rank brought there to enjoy themselves. Not only enemies, but friends, of France were entertained and secretly photographed while making love in the plush rooms.

For rendering an important service to France, the proprietress was protected and permitted to flourish. There was even gossip that she had been secretly awarded the French Legion of Honor.

The house was beautiful and the girls were lovely and talented. I always thought it would be the place to set a great musical — the plot would involve all the heads of state who gathered there after the NATO meetings, and would solve the real problems of the cold war in a bordello with the help of the madam presiding as Secretary General.

Another story I enjoyed about houses of ill repute involved Édouard Herriot, President of the National Assembly. He was descending the stairs of one when he was met by a member of the Assembly. The member bowed and said, "Bonsoir, Monsieur le Président."

The next day, Herriot called everyone in his party together and said, "If you meet your president in a whorehouse — you do not address him as Monsieur le Président, nor do you say bonjour, monsieur. Do you know what to say?"

They all shook their heads.

He said, "You say *nothing*, you stupid asses — nothing at all."

I enjoyed collecting stories concerning great French love affairs. A salesman at Cartier's in Paris was a wonderful source. He related incidents at the store that even De Maupassant couldn't make up. One concerned a beautiful woman who came in one day and tried on a diamond bracelet.

"How much is it?" she asked.

He told her the French equivalent of $30,000.

She said, "I'm going to bring in two gentlemen separately. In each case, when I ask the price, you are to tell me the bracelet is fifteen thousand."

My friend, the salesman, did as he was told. First the woman brought in her lover, and the Cartier man told him the bracelet was $15,000. Then she brought in her husband, and the salesman repeated the same figure. The deal was made — each man put up $15,000 and the woman could wear it anytime she wanted to.

I was not witness to the following story, but I like to believe it was true.

A wealthy lover gave his lady friend, who was married to someone else, a gorgeous fur coat. The woman tried it on and went wild with joy. The only problem was how to explain it to her husband.

Then she had an idea. She took it to the Gare St-Lazare in a large white box and checked it into a locker. She went home, and in the course of the evening said to her husband, "I just found this railroad check on the sidewalk. Why don't you stop by on your way home from work and see if it has any value."

The next day, the husband took the check and on his way home he stopped by the Gare St-Lazare and turned it in. He opened the white box and saw the beautiful coat. He grabbed a taxi and took it to his mistress and gave it to her. Then he bought an umbrella and took it home. He said to his wife, "This is all there was."

I personally was part of a French story, not just the recipient of a tale. I called a radio taxi at ten o'clock at night. The driver was laughing.

"What's so funny?" I asked.

"I just had a fare at rue Richelieu who told me to take him to the Gare de l'Est. Suddenly, over the radio, the dispatcher called for a taxi to go to the same address where I had just picked up the man. The fare said, 'Turn around.'

" 'What about your train?' I asked the man.

"He yelled, 'Turn around.'

"As we pulled up, the man's wife was standing at the curb, all dolled up, waiting for her taxi. The man jumped out of my cab, grabbed her by the arm, and dragged her into the apartment, screaming, 'You could have had the decency to wait until my train left the station!' "

The only drawback to taking Ann with me on my trips was that I couldn't cover a story the way I wanted to. With Ann along I had to worry about her hairdresser, the proper people we would be seeing that night, and make sure we didn't wander into dark alleys in unfamiliar places.

Ann was sympathetic to my problems, but at the same time she was getting tired of telling everyone that I couldn't be at a party because I was on a Ferris wheel in Vienna with Orson Welles.

The irony of celebrity marriage, at least from a male viewpoint, is that women are attracted to men for their glamorous jobs but get very resentful after the honeymoon, because their men are still doing the same exciting things they did before, and don't have time for them.

My most oft-repeated line to Ann when we had a fight was, "You knew what I was like when you married me."

I must have used it a thousand times.

Ann rarely complained about my absences, but there were arguments. They weren't over women or money — but over the lack of time I was spending at home. I had no defense except that I had to think of my career, and I couldn't become famous if I stayed in the children's nursery.

So in my role as a hot-shot columnist, I constantly missed the kids' birthday parties, their appearances in school plays, and even Father's Day. I look back and think how many family celebrations I excluded myself from in order to cover people who meant absolutely nothing to me.

Sometimes I wonder if this was one of the reasons I was using Ann and the kids as material for my column. It was a kind of compensation for not being with them more often. I don't recall feeling particularly guilty about this until the children had grown up and they told me what huge blocks of their lives I had missed. Years later, when I read Ann's diaries, I found out that she had not been too happy about being the butt of my jokes in the pieces I wrote.

Many of my friends stationed abroad were living the same kind of double life. We were constantly entertaining, going out every night, getting on and off planes and trains — but were rarely at home with our families. Visitors expected us to be at their disposal morning, noon, and night.

In spite of her mild complaining, however, Ann was tremendously supportive in my work and the greatest of cheerleaders. She bragged about me to everyone, and while treating me sometimes like a child who didn't know how to tell time, she was very much in love with me and I with her. It was a perfect fit, because we seemed to enjoy the French living, our children, and the fact we had one of the most envied lifestyles of any Americans on the Continent.

Sometimes our social lives defied description. I particularly enjoyed consorting with the Rothschilds, because as a foster child in Queens, New York, I had had a fantasy that I was really a Rothschild and had been kidnapped by my nanny, and sold to my father, a curtain maker in the United States. At the end of the dream, I was rescued by a French detective sent over by the Rothschilds to find me.

In those days, one aspect of my life that we never questioned were the press junkets. Today they would be frowned upon, but in the fifties it was considered part of the job. Ann often accompanied me on these. She loved the trips, because she could be with me and see different parts of the world at the same time. She and I attended the opening of every new Hilton and Sheraton hotel between Spain and Cairo.

One of the most memorable junkets was the opening of the Cairo Hilton in 1959. Conrad Hilton chartered a TWA plane and invited all his friends to his opening. Hiltons were sprouting up all over the place, and the *Trib* said nothing about Conrad picking up the tab. A few years after, the *Trib* began to get squeamish about all the hospitality, as well as the favors the hotel public relations people expected in return, and asked me to cut back on my junkets. This was fine with me, because in exchange for a trip, I felt obligated to say something nice about a place, whether I liked it or not.

Our guest list might not sound impressive today, but at the time we considered it the A-list for hotel openings. We had people like Hedda Hopper, Ann Miller, Earl Wilson and his wife, Rosemary, Bob Considine, Carol Channing, Jinx Falkenburg, actress Terry Moore, and Hilton and son.

One morning, I was standing in the lobby of the Cairo Hilton, when I noticed a man whispering to the manager and looking at me. They both came over. "We would be honored if you would address our students at the university tomorrow."

"You don't want me," I said. "Get Conrad Hilton."

"No, we want you."

"All right," I said modestly.

"What's your name?" the man asked.

The next day, I was driven to the university gymnasium, where five thousand students were noisily awaiting my arrival. I took one look at them and realized that I had bitten off more than I could chew.

I was not certain when they had last heard a distinguished Jewish speaker, so I begged the emcee not to mention the fact that I had been raised in the Hebrew Orphan Asylum.

I got up to speak, and there was a roar from the crowd. I told them that I was on a junket, and that Mr. Hilton was paying all my expenses to visit Cairo — hoping in exchange that I would write something nice about his hotel, which by the way wasn't working that well at the moment. I illustrated my point by telling them that on the previous day I had sent my suit out to be pressed for the evening, as well as my shoes to be shined. I kept calling down in the evening, inquiring where my suit was. By eight, I was furious — I called Housekeeping. "Where is my suit?" I wanted to know. "It's coming," the man replied. "And, by the way, where are my shoes?" The answer was, "What do you want your shoes for, if you don't have your suit?"

Another roar from the crowd. I was off to a good start. The students liked the idea of getting negative information on the Hilton. In one of Cairo's many riots, the student body had set a torch to the famed Shepherd's Hotel and burned it down. So I told them that if they were unhappy about the way things were going politically, to pass up torching the Hilton, because the money came from the Egyptian Social Security fund, and it had been constructed with materials that wouldn't burn. I listed the other hotels in town that were British- and German-owned and much more flammable.

This was very popular. After that, I described what an American columnist did and how politicians lived in fear of us. I said Washington politicians played with the truth, and no matter what they told us, they denied it the next day. (I heard later the U.S. Embassy sent a cable back home denying any role in my speaking at the university.)

Most of the questions from the students concerned America's policy in the Middle East.

Whenever the subject of Israel came up, I told them things were happening at the moment that I just couldn't talk about, but Egypt would be the big winner. I was sure the Israeli intelligence people monitoring my lecture had serious problems figuring out where the hell I was getting my information.

I received a standing ovation at the end of my talk, especially after I suggested that they double their rates for foreign ships going through the Suez Canal.

Ann knew what I was doing, and she was pacing the lobby, wondering if she would ever see me again. "It was a snap," I assured her. "They asked me to come back next month and teach a course in advanced Molotov cocktails."

Another one of my Hilton junkets was to Istanbul. We were flying in a TWA plane, which in those days had sleeping berths for overseas flights. One of Hilton's guests, the wife of a member of the board of directors, had consumed a great deal of alcohol. The flight attendants had to lift her into her bunk against her wishes. Five minutes later, she called out that she wanted to go to the bathroom. Hilton told her to go to sleep.

Two minutes later, something ominous started trickling down from the berth onto Conrad Hilton's head. I observed this from several seats away, and it is impossible to describe the look on the man's face. What made the situation even more surreal was that nobody on the plane said a word — not then or the next morning.

I went to Israel several times, and since I am one of the chosen people, I enjoyed it more than those of other religious persuasions. Perhaps because it was a pioneer country, I found the Israelis short on humor and very defensive about criticism from the outside world. I concluded that the best way to visit the country was to keep my mouth shut and always tell my tour guides how impressed I was with everything they showed me. These included rocks, piles of sand, and broken water pipes. The intensity of their pride was such that, one evening, I was standing on a hill in Jerusalem after a full day of sightseeing and exclaiming at every stone between Tel Aviv and the holy city, when off in the distance I saw a gold-domed church glittering in the sunset.

I pointed at it, and said, "What is that marvelous church over there?"

The guide said impatiently, "Who knows? It's just some damn church."

The first time I visited Israel, I looked up some relatives I had never met named the Kupermans, who lived in Netanya. I called them and was immediately invited to attend their son's wedding.

I showed up and was seated at a place of honor next to the father. While the guests were dancing, his eyes became moist, and he put his arm around my shoulder, and with the other arm, swept over the crowd of two hundred people. "You see all of them. They're all hers," he said, pointing to his wife. Then he hugged me and said, "But you're mine."

The highlight of one visit took place when Ann and I were invited to open the Tel Aviv Sheraton Hotel. The Israeli Army offered to fly me in a helicopter, and I chose to visit the Dead Sea with her. At that moment, they were digging in the caves in the mountains facing Masada, where in 70 A.D. many religious Jews had taken refuge from the Romans.

The caves had been inaccessible for centuries, and the artifacts remained intact, hidden under four or five feet of bat dung.

The army told the antiquities people at Hebrew University that they could have one last crack at the caves before they were sealed for security reasons.

Professor Yigael Yadin, a retired general and one of the country's greatest archaeological experts, was in charge of the dig where we landed in the helicopter. The previous night, one of his volunteer students had made a discovery of scrolls, mirrors, combs, cloth, and candle holders. All of the booty was spread out on the top of the mountain. Yadin showed us everything, and even had the volunteer display his prize for making the discovery — a bottle of French cognac.

Then Yadin said to us, "Would you take the find back in the helicopter, because it will be much safer than putting it on a truck? The scrolls are particularly fragile."

I agreed, and everything was placed in two large Campbell Soup cardboard cartons and tied with string. I carried them to the plane with great care. Proof that all this did happen appears in Yadin's book on the scrolls. He included a photo of me lugging the precious find to the helicopter.

Nowadays when I am on the lecture circuit, I try to work this story in at every opportunity. I say, which is absolutely true, "Carrying the scrolls back to Jerusalem not only gave me a chance to play a small part in a great archaeological discovery — but it also gave me something to read on the plane."

One of the more controversial pieces I wrote about Israel concerned the fact that the U.S. claimed Israel had built an atomic plant outside Beersheba, which violated promises made to Washington that it would not build nuclear weapons.

Israel denied this and maintained that the plant was for the manufacture of textiles for men's clothes. I wrote that the U.S. had decided to check it out, and sent one of its employees there to have a suit made.

The Israelis got wind of the plan and immediately transformed a room with three-foot leaded walls into a fitting room.

The Israeli scientists put pins all over their sleeves to look like tailors. When the American diplomat was ushered in and said he wanted a suit, a scientist said, "You've come to the right place.

We have cobalt blue suits, and uranium brown vests, and double-breasted pin-striped particle models. Shimson, take the man's measurements."

Shimson took a Geiger counter and started yelling out, "Nine-eight-seven-six-five-four-three-two-one."

"Enough with the jokes, Shimson, the man wants a suit."

The American diplomat said, "These fitting rooms seem well-protected."

The scientist said, "Our customers like privacy, and there is so much activity around here we don't like things to pile up."

Shimson said, "He has a U-235 waist."

The American said, "I think the lapels are too wide."

"Don't worry. We'll smash them down for you."

"Do you have any camel-hair swatches I could look at?"

"We do better than that in Beersheba. Here we bring in the whole camel." One of the scientists ran out and brought in a camel.

"Can I charge it?"

Shimson said, "Negative or positive?"

The measurements were made, and

the scientist said, "Your suit will be ready in a week, unless we have some fallout from it."

"Or," said Shimson, "the plant explodes from all our work."

The best part was that the Israeli newspapers were not permitted to write about the Beersheba plant, so all of them were delighted to quote my words from the *Herald Tribune*, which confirmed the plant, even in satirical form.

American correspondents led a glamorous life. We were received very well throughout Europe, especially because most governments wanted good press (and money) from the United States.

In my quest for off-beat stories, I thought I had found the big one in 1958 when I read in the paper that the Soviets had announced the opening up of their roads for the first time, and tourists would be permitted to drive to Moscow.

It was a dream come true — all my life I had wanted to see Mother Russia from a car. This isn't exactly true. The way I have always felt about the Soviet Union is that if you visit it, you have to take it one steppe at a time.

I had no desire to drive myself, so I went to Chrysler and persuaded them to lend me a beautiful Imperial and a chauffeur. I told them that my plan was to travel as a rich American plutocrat and ride in the backseat with hampers of caviar and foie gras, just as the Party members imagined all of us traveled. They agreed, and as a companion I invited my friend Peter Stone (the man who broke the six-minute Louvre).

We started in Paris, stopped in Vienna to be fêted by friends, then drove across Czechoslovakia and on to Poland. The Imperial was the Marilyn Monroe of automobiles. Everywhere we went, people gathered around the car, inspecting the engine, kicking the tires, and crawling underneath the suspension.

"What do you do to own a car like this?" I was asked.

"I am a newspaperman."

"Do all newspapermen own automobiles such as this?"

"All newspapermen I know do. William Randolph Hearst, Henry Luce, Arthur Sulzberger, Jock Whitney, and Joseph Pulitzer."

It was on this trip that I had an

unforgettable horse-racing experience. We were in Warsaw on a Sunday, and I asked the concierge of our hotel what there was to do on the Sabbath.

He said, "Go to the race track." He gave us instructions on how to get there. When we arrived, there was a crowd of about three thousand people. They looked like bettors in any country — some were studying their forms, others were waiting to wager at the windows. Peter and I played numbers rather than horses. Suddenly the bell rang and everyone rushed to the rail. We looked — but there were no horses.

Then the winners were posted: 3-4-6. Some people cheered, others tore up their tickets.

I said to Peter, "Don't say anything."

The next race was the same. The bell rang, the spectators rushed to the rail — no horses — and the winners went up. This was too much, so we asked people near us if anyone spoke French or English. A man said he did speak English. "What's going on?" Peter asked him. "Where are the horses?"

"They're in Cracow," the man replied. "We have only one string, so one week they race in Cracow and one week they race in Warsaw."

"Okay," said Peter, "that makes sense, but if there are no horses, why does everyone rush to the rail?"

The man said, "Where would you go?"

The trip was an adventure into the Dark Ages. We were among the first tourists given permission to drive through the Iron Curtain. In place after place, the roads were almost impassable, and there were no maps available to show us the way. Guide books did not exist for drivers, and even the ditches were military secrets. The Chrysler was a bigger draw than a movie star.

In Brno so many people surrounded the Imperial that the police removed a trolley car from the barn and put the Chrysler inside, so the car would be out of sight. April was a particularly bad time for the roads, and our car got stuck in the snow in Eastern Poland. We borrowed a horse from a farm to pull us out. I printed a photo of it with my article, which I captioned, "Poland adds one more horse to Chrysler horsepower." The Chrysler people were furious with the picture, because they had donated the vehicle, and showing it being pulled out of the snow by a Polish horse did nothing for sales in the United States.

On the road outside Warsaw, we picked up a Polish boy of about thirteen. I offered him a brownie Peter's mother, Hilda, had baked for us. When the boy got out, Peter accused me of making a terrible mistake. "He was a plant by the Secret Police to find out how many brownies we really brought into the country."

I said he was wrong. "He really wanted the ride, and you can't refuse someone food, even if he is a member of the Young Communist League. Besides, if Poland succeeds in taking over the world, the kid will become a minister and he will remember our kindness and invite us to sit next to him at a May Day Parade."

To this day, Peter and I argue about the brownie, and if the boy really wanted it for himself or the State.

When we got to the border, the Polish guards checked our passports and pointed out that we had overstayed our visit by one day. They were very stern. Finally, they called their captain, who said in English, "You remained in Poland twenty-four hours longer than you were supposed to. Why?"

I told him, "Captain, you will understand this. Yesterday was Easter Sunday and we didn't want to go to the Soviet Union and spend it in an atheist country."

The Poles always have been more Catholic than the Pope, so I gambled the captain would buy the story. He winked at us and said to his men, "Let them through."

The road we took led us through Brest, Smolensk, and Minsk. In Smolensk, a man asked us how much the car cost. We gave him the price in rubles. He took out a fistful of money from his pocket and said, "I'll buy it."

The crowds were enormous wherever we went. I was carrying a Polaroid camera, and in Minsk I started taking pictures of the people and handing out the prints. One loyal Party member shouted, "The Soviets make cameras just like that, too."

"Oh," I said. "Where are they?"

"They don't work."

We arrived in Moscow at the Hotel Metropole and, thanks to the car, we were greeted like Armand Hammer. The room was freezing, and we knew the place was bugged when Peter yelled into a radiator, "Don't the friggin' Russians have any heat at all?"

Fifteen minutes later, the room was warm.

Khrushchev was riding high when we visited Moscow, and we met him because we flew an American flag from the Chrysler and had a uniformed chauffeur at the wheel. We pulled up to the Sports Plaza, the Moscow version of Madison Square Garden, and walked right into the hall, where we were escorted to the diplomatic section. According to an interpreter, Khrushchev was talking dirty, which he did quite a bit. Whenever we asked what he said, the diplomat told us he could not tell us, because the language was so awful.

After the speech, a Russian reporter wanted to know what we thought of it. Peter said, "If he didn't use such filthy language, he would be another Billy Graham."

The reporter looked perplexed.

I told him, "This is the highest compliment you can give a leader after a political speech."

Pravda, one of the leading Soviet newspapers, was not pleased when my columns on the visit were published. They assigned one of their top writers to deal with my series. He accused me of fabricating most of it. For example, I wrote that I saw wolves between Minsk and Smolensk and the local authorities had ordered them to eat me. The *Pravda* writer refuted this, and claimed that anyone who had any knowledge of the Soviet Union would know that there were no wolves between Minsk and Smolensk, and if there were, they would be too smart to attack an automobile.

Furthermore, *Pravda* noted, I had reported the scene of my car being stuck in the snow and how Soviet truck drivers had stopped to pull it out. I said it was a wonderful example of Soviet-American cooperation. The Russians pulled and the Americans took photos. How ungrateful could I be?

The writer also hit me hard over my assertion that the restaurants were so badly run that I almost starved to death on my visit. I'd reported that all the good tailors had departed in 1905 and all the trained waiters in 1917. The only people left were slave laborers, and all they did was play card games in the back of the restaurant while refusing to go near the tables.

I said that the kitchen committee caucused every day to protest their lack of equipment. Rice was the favorite dish in the Metropole but could not be ordered unless approved by a machine tractor station on the Black Sea. Three days later, the rice was shipped to the Central Committee in Moscow, and three days later served to the customer without a fork.

In summing up his rebuttal, the *Pravda* writer said, "Before his departure, Buchwald vowed to write only the truth. But he wrote only lies, which he sucked out of his finger in the office of the New York *Herald Tribune*."

Irony of ironies — despite the attack, *Pravda* kept using my columns.

I have returned to the Soviet Union several times since then — once with Ann. She was frightened silly the entire time we were there. The first night, she cried, and the second night, she cried — the truth is, she cried every night. The room described as "Grand Deluxe" was a third-rate closet in every respect, and to make matters worse, a forbidding-looking woman maintained a vigil on the floor. She handed us our keys and reported on everything we did.

When I joked about us being followed, Ann believed me and kept looking over her shoulder. Usually she said she liked everything during our travels, even pretending many times she loved a place when she didn't. But she never faked her fear of Russia.

During my trip with Ann, I complained to the Russian press that I had not been paid any royalties, despite the fact that they had published my columns and books for years. The chief High Executioner of writers offered to give me rubles and even held a lunch to bestow them on me. I accepted the luncheon, but at the last moment I refused the money, because, I insisted, "The dollar is very, very weak and the ruble is very strong — so I would much prefer to keep the royalties in Moscow, where I can build up a large trust fund with ten percent Russian interest."

The last time I was in the Soviet Union was in 1989, when I was part of a delegation of American writers who were hosted by *Krokodil*, the Soviet humor magazine.

When we arrived at the airport, the Moscow editors greeted us warmly and told us that they had a special treat in store for us. They said we would be the first Americans permitted to go to Chernobyl, the site of the nuclear accident.

I said through an interpreter, "Are you out of your friggin' minds?"

"Why don't you want to go to Chernobyl?"

"Because I don't want to go any place where the best I can hope for is that I will be as healthy when I come out as when I went in."

I really loved so many places that I visited during those years in Paris, but it didn't take long to be down on the Soviet Union. Not only was it gray and foreboding, but the civil servants, from passport officials to hotel concierges, were recruited from the cruelest groups in the country. The system required people with authority to dump on those who had none. It was a country where everyone had to have a piece of paper, and that paper had to be stamped, and then taken somewhere to be exchanged for another piece of paper that also had to be stamped. The people checking whether the paper was stamped or not could be bribed. Luxuries were available on the black market — the bureaucrats controlled the system and drove it into the ground.

On one visit, we were shown a large apartment complex in Moscow with no windows in it. The glass had been ordered from the Ukraine, but the people who made it wouldn't ship it to the apartment house in Moscow because they'd gotten a better deal from a State construction company in Leningrad. So the apartments stood empty, another tribute to some idiotic minister's five-year plan.

The whole country seemed to be filled with paranoia. I took a Soviet journalist to lunch and warmed up to him when he told me all the problems he had as a Jew. That evening, I was relating my conversation to a U.S. Embassy attaché. He said, "We know him well. He works for the KGB."

"Why would he unload on me?"

"Because his job is to find out where you stand on issues. The man *is* a Jew, and it's possible he is gathering the intelligence against his will. But he still reports directly to the Secret Police."

In spite of my disenchantment with

their country and its political system, the Russians continued to print my columns — particularly when I attacked the U.S. government. I was once hosted at *Izvestia*, and I said to the editor, "You always use my articles when I make fun of my own country. Are you going to use my columns now that I'm making fun of the USSR?" He smiled and said, "We don't have room."

One day, I received a call from the State Department, and a man said, "Do you know the Russians used your column this morning?" and I said, "Stop them."

After one piece appeared in the Soviet papers, I was asked to comment on my feelings and I said, "I don't care if the Russians use my articles or not, and I don't care if they pay me or not — because I really work for the CIA and my column is a code to our agents in Moscow. Every third word is a message to one of our people there."

The Russians reported in *Pravda*, "We always knew Buchwald worked for the CIA, and that is why we always scrambled that third word."

One of my fun trips was to the Belgian

Congo, now known as Zaire. I persuaded Gordon Manning of *Collier's* magazine to let me do a piece titled "Coward in the Congo," which was a spoof of big-game hunting as practiced by writers such as Ernest Hemingway and Robert Ruark. My premise for going was that no one could be considered a serious writer anymore unless he had hired a white hunter and had killed a beast whose head he could hang in his library.

Manning said okay and assigned a photographer named Joe Covello to accompany me. He told Covello to shoot for a cover, just in case.

We flew to Stanleyville and then continued by jeep into the Ituri forest, where the Pygmies lived. The Belgians had arranged for us to have one of their crack white hunters and two dozen local people to take us on safari.

I was dressed to kill and provided with porters, and a chair in which to be carried by bearers. I convinced myself that nobody out there could tell the difference between me and Hemingway. On the first day, I told the white hunter that I hated shooting and I didn't want to kill anything, but since we needed a cover picture I would appreciate it if he shot an animal for me.

It didn't seem to bother him, and the next day we went out into the bush. I played the role of the American sportsman, with Covello taking pictures of me all day long. Finally, at a watering hole, we saw a Thomas Cob antelope, and the white hunter knocked him down with one shot.

I went over with Covello to the antelope, and we spent three hours posing for photographs with him in every possible position. The natives didn't know what to make of it, because they had never seen an American so picture-crazy.

Long after I left the Congo, I discovered that events from the safari had followed me. A year later, I was in Paris, and I ran into someone from the Congo and asked him how things were going down there.

He said, "Just great. You know you're a legend in the country."

"How's that?"

"They don't know your name, but they still talk about the American tourist who had his white hunter shoot this Thomas Cob and then spent three hours posing for photographs with it in the bush."

In addition to my white hunter experience, I decided that another adventure was needed to help me in my quest to become a great writer — Pamplona, and running with the bulls struck me as an essential experience.

As budding authors, several of my Paris friends felt the same way. To all of us, it seemed a Hemingway thing to do. So in 1959, I boarded a train from Paris and went to Spain.

I was among the brave ones. I wore a beret and a red bandanna and sneakers, and I drank wine from a leather *bota.* The idea of running with the bulls is as follows: You eat dinner at midnight and you stay awake anticipating the event, and as dawn comes, you get ready for the race, which might mean that you would be gored in such a way as to lose the family jewels. The admiring camp followers drank from our *botas* and kissed us tenderly. The bull runners kept hitting each other on the arms, and we talked fluent Hemingway.

The race was ready to begin. We had a lead of a block on the bulls. When the gun went off, we raced through the narrow streets, with angry bulls pounding behind us. If you weren't fast enough, the best thing to do was duck into a doorway and let them race by.

The real danger came when you were racing into the tunnel that led into the arena. It was very narrow, and if someone tripped, everyone went flying.

I ran fast, just like Papa would have wanted me to. I got through the tunnel and into the bull ring, where thousands cheered. I ran around the ring, tipping my beret to all my admirers. I had proved once and for all I was a man.

With me that day, also taking their bows, were George Plimpton, Peter Matthiessen, Irwin Shaw, Herb Kretzmer, Allen Ginsberg, and Gregory Corso. The morning would stay with us all our lives, and we would be blood brothers until the last bull in Pamplona faced death in the afternoon.

Our women admirers were so proud of us they toasted us from the same wine sacs, holding them above their heads and letting the wine pour down their beautiful throats. For some of us this was a bigger turn-on than reading *For Whom the Bell Tolls* in a sleeping bag.

"Was it good?" my Scandinavian companion asked.

I told her, "It was very good."

"Was it as good as making love to Rita Hayworth?"

"Yes, but different."

"Had you been gored, I would have licked your wounds."

"A lot of Scandinavian girls like to do that."

After reading that, Ann offered to do something for me, too, but it wasn't quite as much fun.

Chapter 8

The Movies and Me

People always love to read about movie stars and their lives, and so in the old days I would go to every film festival I was invited to. All our expenses were paid and we stayed in the best hotels.

The two major film festivals were Cannes and Venice. When it came to motion pictures, Europe was so much more interesting than America. I had the impression that it was inhabited by nothing but creative scoundrels. In addition to the French and Italian producers, there were exiled Bulgarian, Romanian, Russian, and Armenian promoters trying to raise enough production money to pay their hotel bills. If someone else picked up their check at a sidewalk café, they considered it a very good day.

The entertainment at the film festivals took place outside the halls on the

Croisette. There were fierce arguments over who owed what to whom. Accusations were hurled at people for stealing other people's stories, and planting items with the press concerning what productions the wheelers intended to make next was the order of the day.

Sam Spiegel, who made *Lawrence of Arabia* and *The African Queen*, was a benign rogue, as was the showman Mike Todd. They were generous with their friends but were unwilling to pay the people who worked for them. If you wanted caviar and champagne, you were welcome to have it. A cruise on a yacht was no problem. But they were loathe to compensate anyone in their employ.

Al Hix, a friend from USC, was doing publicity for Sam in Paris on a film called *Melba*. Since I had helped Hix land the job, he complained to me that Sam was four weeks behind in his pay, which was $200 a week.

That evening, I stopped by Sam's suite at the Hôtel George-V. The waiter rolled in the caviar and vodka on a trolley.

"How much is a can of caviar here?" I asked.

Sam, thinking I was being social, said,

"Five hundred dollars."

"Then," I shouted, "why the hell don't you pay Hix the money you owe him?"

Sam was hurt. "That's the trouble with being a producer. Everybody wants something from you."

The most money I ever made at one time during my stay in Europe was when I wrote a novel based on my experience with American gangsters who had been deported to Italy, and then sold it to the movies.

One day, a scar-faced man, wearing a grimy fedora, walked into my office and said his name was Frank Frigenti, and he was a deported thug from New York.

Frank said that he had been sent to me by my good friend Ben Bradlee. He told me that he had tried to sell Bradlee on what the life of an Italian deportee from the U.S. was like in Naples. But Bradlee, playing a typical Ivy League trick, had told Frigenti it sounded more like my kind of story. The gangster came into my office and said he would sell his story for $500.

I offered him $20 and he took it.

Before he revealed what he knew, he showed me his credentials, which included a yellow newspaper clipping saying that he had murdered his mother-in-law.

Frigenti said that he had been deported to Italy because he was of Italian birth, and the U.S. was forcing the Italians to take all their gangsters back. Many wound up in Naples, where they found the living tough. "The only thing we can do," he said, "is deal in drugs and women. I make my living taking Americans to back alleys where they get cheated on fake Rolex watches."

I wrote everything down, and it made a good story.

Not long after it appeared, I received a letter from a deportee in Naples claiming that Frigenti was a lying rat, who had been driven out of Naples by the law-abiding deportees who wanted no part of him. The letter read, "In reference to Frank Frigenti, he is a faker and a stool pigeon. We chased him out of Naples after we made sure he spent twenty-six days in the hospital for snitching on the other deportees. He knows Al Capone and others only through the magazines. He reads the *Police Gazette* and then sells his stories about gangsters to suckers like you. His

337

stories have made our lives very detrimental. If you do not believe what I am writing you, I am willing to tell you in front of the punk Frigenti. If we were dealing in dope and women, we would be leading luxurious lives, instead of panhandling tourists when they come out of the American Express office.

"We aren't in drugs and dope, because the Italian gangsters won't let us be. Some of us deportees were born in Italy but taken to the U.S. as infants, and hardly knew Italian. Rather than be in the big time, the only way we can survive is by selling 'genuine' Parker pens to American sailors from the Sixth Fleet. Come down and see for yourself what a deportee has to do to make a living.

"P.S. Even Frigenti's mother will piss on him if she sees him."

I showed the letter to Eric, who suggested it might make a good series. To kill two birds with one stone, I wrote to Lucky Luciano, the Babe Ruth of American gangsters, and I asked if I could interview him. It turned out Luciano loved the *Tribune*, as it was his tie to home. He was familiar with my column, so he agreed to have lunch.

Luciano, one of the most celebrated gangsters of all time, had been in exile in Naples for seven years, after serving ten years of a thirty-to-fifty-year sentence for white slavery.

Somehow — no one knows why — he had been released from prison and deported to Italy. When I saw him, he was very bitter, and told me that the Americans had framed him. He also said he had served the U.S. honorably during World War II by keeping the longshoremen on both coasts from going out on strike.

We met at the Giacomini Restaurant, where Luciano ate every day. He was accompanied by a German shepherd and two heavyset companions who were his bodyguards. I noticed the owner kept all the tables around Luciano empty, and the only ones permitted to sit near us were the two thugs.

Like many top gangsters, Luciano was softspoken and very polite. At the beginning, he told me which comic strips he liked in the *Tribune,* and asked where I got my ideas for my column.

Luciano was full of scorn for U.S. politicians because he said he was being used by the Democrats as a political pawn. He said, "They're making a big deal of the fact that Thomas Dewey arranged for me to leave prison and go to Naples."

This was ironic, because Dewey was responsible for Luciano's original conviction and sending him to Sing-Sing.

"You must be grateful Dewey let you out of prison."

"Yeah, I'm grateful he let me out, but am I supposed to be grateful he put me in?"

It was hard for me to believe that I was sitting at the same table as one of the most notorious gangsters of all time. As a life-time experience, it wasn't in the class with meeting Joe DiMaggio, but it came close. Luciano didn't look like a killer, nor did he act like one. He was a fastidious eater and an engaging conversationalist. I could not wait to write back home to my father and say, "Guess who bought me lunch in Naples."

The big news from the interview was that Luciano was thinking about writing a book. I said, "I thought your people pay you so you won't write a book."

"I wouldn't write it about my friends. I'd blow the whistle on all the legitimate office-holders who are the real crooks in the country."

Luciano told me his pet peeve was that he had been accused by the U.S. of being involved in the narcotics business in Italy.

"They got no proof and they're persecuting me. I had gambling joints and I bootlegged booze, but I never got into dope. Narcotics is a lousy business. It ruins people's lives."

No one approached our table at lunch, but word had spread Lucky was there again, and people were staring through the window. He said, "Did you know the U.S. Navy put out an order to the sailors not to ask for my autograph?"

When we finished lunch, I said, "Mr. Luciano, I just bought this coral necklace for my wife, it cost me one hundred dollars. Did I get screwed?"

He threw it over to his bodyguards. "The kid says he paid a hundred for this. What do you think?" A bodyguard examined it and said, "Whoever charged him a hundred for this crap should be shot."

"Damn," I said.

"What are you complaining about?" Luciano said. "They screw me like this every day."

As we said farewell, he said, "Hey, you know all that stuff I said about narcotics being a lousy business. You better not print that. I still got a lot of pals in New York who might be in the business."

From Luciano, I went on to meet the deportees, in a rundown café facing the port. They were a sorry lot, and they were bitter at the raw deal they claimed to have gotten. "We didn't do nothing" was the refrain. "And this is what they do to us."

The most amazing thing was how patriotic they were, and how much they insisted that they loved the United States. One told me he'd spent thirty days in jail because an Italian gangster had said the U.S. Navy was made up of nothing but "queers." The deportee claimed the Italian police made the American gangsters into their personal punching bags.

One exile told me the Italian mobsters were particularly annoyed with the deportees, because their presence put the heat on Naples and there were more police stationed there than the city needed.

So the deportees hung out with each other and, unlike Lucky Luciano, whom they all envied because he lived in a penthouse overlooking Naples Bay, they scrounged for a living and considered themselves men without countries.

To a man, they detested Frank Frigenti, and when I asked, "Did he or did he not kill his mother-in-law?" Petey Onofrio, the author of the letter, said, "If he did, it was a crime of passion."

When my column appeared which quoted the Naples boys on Frigenti, I was still in Italy. Frigenti showed up at the *Trib* in a rage. Sylvan Barnett, the general manager at the time, saw him, and Frigenti said my column had hurt his chances of making a living in France and he had a good mind to do away with Barnett. He left the office. The good news was that after reading the *Trib*, the French police picked him up and shipped him off to Italy.

While talking to these people, it occurred to me that there was a novel in all this — the deportees on the bottom of the heap and Lucky Luciano on the top. They were all in their own way part of Americans abroad, and so I chose Sicily as the perfect setting for my tale.

I called my novel *A Gift from the Boys*, the hero being a Luciano type who is being deported to Italy. His mob assumes he'll be back soon, when his appeal is upheld. In order to make his departure less painful, they give him a showgirl as a going-away present (of course I was thinking Marilyn Monroe).

The main character believes he's going to Rome, but instead he is sent to the town of La Coma, a miserable fishing village in Sicily, where he was born — which is not what he had in mind.

I researched the story in Sicily for a month, and whatever I uncovered was far wilder than anything I could invent. For example, the owner of the fish cannery was a mean, elderly countess who cheated the fishermen in the town in every way she could. This character really lived, and I visited the cannery and talked to the people who were at her mercy.

In my story, I wanted my Luciano figure kidnapped by a Sicilian bandit and held for ransom. A real bandit — Giuliano, a Robin Hood of the area — had existed. I modeled this character on him. For authenticity, I asked to interview someone who had been kidnapped by Giuliano, and my researcher found the Duke of Palermo. He told us he had been abducted from his car on a road and spirited away into the mountains. The duke had been outraged, and said if they were going to keep him, they had to feed him well.

"What do you want to eat?" Giuliano asked him.

The duke provided a week-long menu of lobster and fresh seafood, lamb and steak, and a special type of pasta only made in one shop in Palermo.

The requested dishes were provided during the stay while the ransom was being gathered. The duke told us it was complicated, because he had a mistress, and his wife was so furious with him she wouldn't pay anything from the family funds.

Finally, the duke's lawyer persuaded the bank to let him have the money.

The lawyer climbed the mountain and delivered the funds in a large briefcase. Giuliano's men counted it and then told their kidnapper it was all there.

The duke got up to leave, but Giuliano stopped him and said, "Wait a minute

— the food is not included."

The bandit handed his victim another bill for $2,000.

I also visited Giuliano's home in the mountains of Sicily. His mother and sister still lived in the house. I told them through my interpreter that I was doing a film on Giuliano so the whole world would know what a good man he had been. They cried as I talked. I then asked to visit his grave. We took off through the dusty streets. It was pointed out to me that there were no men in the village — they were all in jail. When we got to the cemetery, we passed a grave, and both the mother and sister spat on it. Then we arrived at the outlaw's grave, and mother and daughter knelt to pray. Afterwards, they got up, and when we passed the same grave as before, the two women spat again.

"Find out what all that was about," I said to my guide.

She talked to the mother, and then replied, "The grave that they spat on was Giuliano's cousin who turned him in to the police. They said they will spit on it until they die."

When I finished the book, I gave it to

Cary Grant, who liked it and said he wanted to play Luciano. That's all director Stanley Donen needed to know, and he bought it for $50,000. But Stanley messed the script up so badly that it bore no resemblance to the book, and Cary Grant wanted nothing to do with the script.

It was a typical Hollywood disaster story. Donen hired a fine writer named Arnold Shulman to write the script. The minute Stanley bought the book, he refused to talk to me. I know the details because Shulman told them to me.

Donen wanted Sophia Loren to play the gift. This complicated things, since Sophia was Italian and was not too believable as a showgirl from the United States.

Donen had the solution. "Why does Sophia have to be a gift? Why can't she meet the hero in Sicily in a café and then fall in love with him?"

Shulman said, "But the title of the book is *A Gift from the Boys*."

Donen said, "Well, change it. What law is there you can't change a title? Did it ruin *Green Grow the Lilacs* to call it *Oklahoma!*?"

Shulman, who had come to Europe

with a pregnant wife, was at Donen's mercy.

After going down the Sophia Loren road — she turned down the script — Donen came back with another idea. Princess Soraya was all over the papers, as she had recently been divorced by the Shah of Iran because she couldn't produce a male heir. Stanley suggested the heroine be a princess. Donen wanted Frank Barlett, the gangster, to fall in love with the princess, now played by Ingrid Bergman, and rather than a comedy, the film was to be a tragic love story.

It was at this moment that Ingrid Bergman told Donen to stuff it.

Several years later, Donen made a film titled *Surprise Package* with Yul Brynner and Mitzi Gaynor. The action took place in Greece. It was one of the year's great stinkers, and when I saw it, I didn't know whether to laugh or cry. So I cried.

But I had made $50,000, so everyone told me not to worry. The only real satisfaction I got out of it was that Bradlee, who'd sent me Frigenti, demanded a 50 percent finder's fee. I told him, "You don't give someone a finder's fee when he sends you someone who can kill you."

Speaking of Ingrid Bergman, she had become a friend over the years, and I was there when she was making *Stromboli* in Italy. She'd left her Swedish husband, Dr. Peter Lindstrom, and taken up with director Roberto Rossellini and had his child. At the time, more was made of this than the U.S. dropping the atomic bomb on Hiroshima. The world was outraged, and so was the Senate of the United States. One member of that august body even demanded Ingrid be denied admission to the United States on the grounds of moral turpitude.

I was sympathetic to Ingrid, because I was also in love with her, and hoped after she got bored with Rossellini, she would turn to me. I knew that she had had tons of letters about her affair, and I asked her if she would allow me to peruse her mail and use excerpts in a piece I was doing for *Look* magazine.

Much to my surprise, and delight, she said yes, and for the next three days, I was holed up in her apartment, examining samples of what amounted to thousands of hate letters from every corner of the globe.

A few excerpts:

"I begged God to show me how to lift you up to decency and he told me, 'Go to the King of Sweden on your knees and beg his forgiveness. Only he has the power to pardon you for having a child out of wedlock.' "

"Get rid of Rausalini [sic] the lousy lover — he stink. The best lover you could have right now is Dr. Peter Lindstrom. If you take up with Rausalini, put your own money in your own account."

"I am Swedish and Lutheran. How much moolah will you and Roberto have to kick in to the Catholic church before they forgive you for your sins?"

While the people who objected to the love affair were virulent, Ingrid also received many letters from supporters who told her she had done a gutsy thing. Like many motion picture stars' scandals of the heart, Ingrid's trespasses were eventually forgiven, and she continued to be one of the finest and most sought-after actresses of our time.

The only frightening part of my episode with the Rossellinis was that

Roberto insisted on driving me to the airport after I finished my research. He had a Maserati and we sailed through Rome at an average 100 miles an hour. As if this wasn't bad enough, he kept showing me with both hands what he would like to do to the people who were condemning Ingrid for her love affair.

Marlene Dietrich was another friend — not an intimate one, but we got along just fine when she came to Paris.

A good example of how people take celebrities for granted was illustrated on the opening night of her stage show in London at the Café de Paris. It was one of the glitziest occasions I had covered.

Princess Margaret was there, along with stars of stage, screen, and the arts. Marlene had never been better. She had an evening gown that you thought you could see through — but you couldn't. Her sultry voice, and the way she made love to everyone in the audience, had the crowd applauding and screaming. Afterwards, I went back to her dressing room, which was filled with flowers.

The "dahlings" were flung all over the place. The hugging and kissing went on incessantly. I sat in the corner, enjoying the adulation she was getting.

But an hour later, I looked around and there was no one there. All those fans and friends were gone. Nobody had bothered to ask Marlene if she had plans after the show.

I finally said, "Would you like to go to supper with me?"

She said she'd love to, and after her evening to remember, I wound up alone with the toast of London. We went to Les Ambassadors, where we sat for hours, talking. The payoff for me was when she began to relate tales of all the men she had slept with and who were good and who were lousy. My favorite story was about the time General Omar Bradley wouldn't allow her to go to the front to entertain troops during World War II. She said, "So I had no choice but to sleep with him." I thought to myself, she got permission to go to the front the hard way.

Another event that brought the war back was when I was invited to go for a ride on an aircraft carrier in the Mediterranean. As a former Marine enlisted man, it was a once-in-a-lifetime treat for me. They flew me off the carrier in a fighter bomber, I supped in the officers' mess, and I wound up sleeping in the captain's cabin. (He had two, one below decks, and one topside, where he slept while I was on board.) They put a lieutenant commander in charge of me, and every time he called me "Sir" my chest swelled, and I thought of Glenn Sullivan (Sully), my Marine Sergeant in VMF 113, who'd constantly told me I had no future in the military.

My cabin was located beneath the ship's catapult, which launched the fighters into the night. Every thirty seconds, it fired, and sounded as if a cannon had gone off in my head.

At two in the morning, I finally got to sleep, when the phone rang, and a voice shouted, "Sir, there is a fire in the galley."

"Well, put the goddamn thing out," I said.

The next morning, I told the captain what I had done, and he said, "I would have said the same thing."

The headquarters for the Sixth Fleet was the lovely town of Villefranche, between Nice and Monaco. The wives of officers of the fleet lived in regal splendor, and to many it was considered the best duty in the world. But like any

American dependent group, some loved it and others could not wait to get back to the U.S.

The whereabouts of ships were top secret and none of the wives were told when their menfolk were coming home. Their only clue was when all the French hookers started showing up in the town's bars. As soon as they were spotted, the wives called each other excitedly, and said, "Praise the Lord — the girls are here, which means our men are coming back."

There was one celebrity I never got to know, though, and it was my own fault. I was on a trip to Monte Carlo. Everyone had gotten off the train in Cannes, and I was alone in my car, except for a woman in the next compartment. We had over an hour to go and we were both standing in the aisle, looking at the Riviera scene as we sped by. Ordinarily, I would have started up a conversation with her, but she was very plain-looking and cold. I did say something like "Bonjour," and she replied in kind.

Finally, the train arrived in Monte Carlo. As I stepped down onto the platform, I noticed that my fellow passenger had thrown her arms around a man I knew named George Schlee. Then he saw me and said, "Art, you know Greta Garbo, don't you?"

I thought to myself, "I could have been a contender."

And then there was Gina Lollobrigida. I was the love of her life, though she'd never admit it. The story goes like this: In the fifties, some of the biggest names on the European scene were the Greek shipowners. They were fabulously wealthy; because of the Suez, their tankers were much in demand. Two of the best known were Stavros Niarchos and Aristotle Onassis. They were related by marriage, having married two sisters whose father owned even more ships. When Stavros married his wife, Eugenia, he said that Onassis asked him to arrange a marriage to her sister, Tina.

The two were archrivals and competed not only in business but in the good life as well. If one had a 300-foot yacht, the other wanted one 301 feet.

Both men entertained lavishly and were much sought after on the free-loading social circuit. One of Onassis's one-upmanship coups was to purchase the shares of the Societé des Bains de Mer, which owned the hotels and casinos in Monte Carlo.

The purchase made the poor boy raised in Argentina one of the most glamorous public figures in the world.

I became personally involved with both men by accident. I received a call from Niarchos, asking me to fly down to his villa at Cap D'Antibes. I told him that because it was a weekend I couldn't get transportation. He said he would send his private plane for me. I told him I would be happy to see him.

When Ann saw me packing, she wanted to know where I was going. I told her, "Stavros has to talk to me and he's sending a private plane. The man drives me crazy."

When I landed at the Nice airport, a uniformed chauffeur was waiting in a Bentley. As I was driven along in splendor, I could only wish the girls I'd lusted for at USC could see me now. I was also trying to figure out what Niarchos wanted from me. Perhaps he had discovered that I was really a Rothschild and wished to sell me a piece of his shipping empire, or maybe he wanted to offer me his island in the Aegean Sea.

No matter what, it had to be big. Greek shipowners don't send airplanes for American paupers who got to Paris courtesy of the G.I. Bill.

Niarchos was waiting for me at the door, and greeted me like a long-lost cousin. I hardly knew the man. We had occasionally shaken hands at parties and exchanged pleasantries. That was the extent of our relationship. He got down to business right away. "Here's what I want from you," he said. "I want you to write a story about that bitch Elsa Maxwell. She claims I'm paying for a masked ball she's giving in Venice and it's a big lie. I want everyone who reads the *Herald Tribune* to know the truth."

Elsa Maxwell was an American who was the self-appointed cruise director for the International Set. One of her roles was as an intermediary acquiring free clothes for the Duchess of Windsor from the Paris fashion houses. Elsa gave parties with other people's money and, while a figure of scorn, was constantly used by those who made fun of her.

I agreed with Niarchos to write that he had nothing to do with the party. Then he said he would take me to lunch at one of the great restaurants on the Riviera, the Bonne Auberge. Driving out in the Bentley, we had to pull aside on the dirt road, because another automobile was coming from the opposite direction.

The approaching car's door opened, and out stepped Elsa Maxwell, who yelled, "Stavros, I ran out of invitations. Do you have any more at the house?"

I looked at Niarchos, and said, "What else should we talk about at lunch?"

Niarchos was steaming. Finally, I said, "Look, I read in *Paris-Match* that you claim you own half of Monte Carlo. You said you and Onassis were supposed to be partners, and he cheated you out of the deal. Let's talk about that."

"It's true," he admitted. "We had a deal. He would own half of the Ritz, which I just bought, and I would get half the shares in Monte Carlo. I'll put it up for mediation. Anyone can arbitrate it — you could arbitrate it if you want to."

"You would let me arbitrate a dispute between you and Onassis?" I said.

"Why not? I appoint you." He was so mad he was serious.

"Okay," I said. "Lend me your Bentley and I'll go see him."

After lunch, the chauffeur drove me to Monte Carlo, where I found Onassis on his yacht, *The Christina.* It was a real boat. Gossip had it that the German shipyards had given it to him as a kickback for several supertankers Onassis had ordered from them.

The Christina had a swimming pool on the deck and a seaplane on board. The thing I remember the most is the six barstools in the bar, which Onassis boasted were covered with leather from only one whale's penis. I told this story to Betsy Drake, Cary Grant's wife, one day, and she said "Moby's Dick?"

When I came on board, Onassis, a very warm person when he wanted to be, threw his arms around me. I repulsed him. "Ari, I am not here as a friend. I am here as an arbitrator. Niarchos says he owns half of Monte Carlo, and he has asked me to judge whether it is true or not."

Onassis exploded. "That son of a bitch. That thief, that rotten ingrate. He owns nothing. We never had a deal and he knows it."

"I thought you would say something

like that. But in order to get the facts, I am going to need more than your denial."

Onassis said, "I'll show you the FBI file on Niarchos and you'll see what a rotten liar he really is. Stay on board as my guest tonight and come to the Red Cross Gala with me. You can be Gina Lollobrigida's escort. I will have my plane fly down from Paris with the file in the morning."

It seemed like a reasonable request, so I stayed. Onassis sent one of his people to find me a tuxedo and put me up in a spacious cabin.

The arbitration was working well, until late in the afternoon, when I called Ann in Paris and tried to explain what was going on.

"I'm a guest on Onassis's yacht, because I've been appointed as mediator between him and Stavros Niarchos over who owns Monte Carlo. I'm calling to tell you that I'm taking Gina Lollobrigida to the Red Cross Ball tonight, and when you see my picture in the paper tomorrow morning with her, you may think I was having a good time, not knowing it was strictly business."

There was dead silence at the other

end of the line. Finally, she said, "Is that all you called me about?"

"How are the kids?"

She hung up on me.

I must say, when Ann was stuck at home and I was on the road covering Venice, Cannes, Monte Carlo, and Capri, it was difficult to report that what I was doing was serious, and that I was not having fun. So I always downplayed my activities. I might say if I was in Deauville covering Frank Sinatra, "It's raining, and Sinatra had this boring party in his suite until six in the morning, and I don't think there is a story here. Thank God you weren't here, because you would have hated every moment of it." Or "Venice isn't what it's cracked up to be — too many boats — too few streets. You're lucky you stayed home."

The Red Cross Ball went well, and because I was sitting at Onassis's table, everyone spoke to me, and patted me on the head.

Gina was frosty. An outsider might think she was wondering why Ari couldn't get her a better escort than a reporter from the *Herald Tribune*, but I knew she was just hiding her feelings about me.

The next morning, Onassis's file on Niarchos was delivered to my cabin, and it was hair-raising. Every crime committed by Niarchos was in the folder, and as I read it I knew that if I ever printed any of it, I would be sued for libel for a zillion Greek drachmas or Swiss francs.

When I saw him at breakfast, Ari said, "Now is that the kind of man I would want for a partner?"

I said, "Let me have one of the motorboats. I'm going to see Niarchos."

I boarded a thirty-five-foot speedboat and went back to Niarchos's villa to report to him. He wanted to know what Onassis had said.

I told him, "Onassis showed me his file on you."

Niarchos screamed, "That swine. You want to see files. I'll show you files." Niarchos went to the safe in his library, opened it, and handed me a folder about the same size as the one Onassis had on him. I found out later both shipowners had ex-CIA agents in their employ, who were paid to find out the dirt on each other.

I sat in the library studying the documents. If anything, the criminal charges on Onassis were worse than the ones Ari showed me on Niarchos. If I printed any of it, Onassis would sue me for libel for zillions of Italian lire or Spanish pesos or even tons of Saudi Arabian oil.

I decided to make one more stab at it by returning to see Onassis and asking him to show me the bill of sale on the Monaco Company.

I said, "I need proof that you have sole title to the place."

He was about to reply, when he looked at me and said, "Wait a minute, wait a minute. You're the one causing all the trouble. Who the hell asked you to get into this?"

"Niarchos."

Ari started screaming. "You bastard journalist. I'm going to call Mrs. Reid and have you fired."

"She won't do it. I am her illegitimate son."

"Why are you doing this to me?"

I made the mistake of saying, "I have to make a living."

Onassis said, "Oh, is that it?" He took a fistful of French francs out of his pocket and said, "How much do you want?"

"I didn't mean that kind of living. I have to do my job."

"Get off the boat. When I buy the *Trib*, you are the first one to get fired."

I left and had to hitch back to Niarchos's villa to pick up my bag.

Despite my efforts, nothing changed — Onassis kept Monte Carlo and Niarchos kept the Ritz.

When I got home, Ann had all the newspaper photos of me and Gina Lollobrigida in front of her. She said, "So what happened?"

I replied, "I took Gina to the Red Cross Ball. She was wearing a white evening gown and an emerald necklace and she talked Italian with the guy on her other side, and never spoke to me all evening. Poor girl. I think her heart was broken."

Ann gave me a look. It reminded me of that time after the running of the bulls . . .

Chapter 9

The Road Back

And then, suddenly, it was over.

In February 1962, I returned to the United States to begin a lecture tour. Ann decided to come with me. One of my stops was Washington, D.C., where I visited old pals, including Ben Bradlee, who gave us a party. Ben was close friends with President Kennedy and knew everyone in the administration. It was a glitzy affair, and Ann and I were dazzled by all the political superstars — Arthur Schlesinger, Bobby and Ethel Kennedy, Walter Lippman, Eunice and Sarge Shriver, senators and congressmen of both parties.

The atmosphere at the party was electric. As I looked around at the guests, I saw that everyone there was a part of the country's present history. To make it even more seductive, they were all extremely nice to us.

The following day, Pierre Salinger invited Ann and me to the White House to attend a press briefing, and then took us to the Oval Office to shake hands with the president, who asked me what I was doing in the United States. I said, "Lecturing." The president spent at least ten minutes of his time with us, which I thought was a lot.

After a week of political stargazing, Ann and I were flying back to Paris.

I said, "I think it's time to go home."

"Why?"

"I'm running stale. I'm repeating myself. I've satirized every nationality in Europe. I want to throw up every time I do another ugly American story. Fourteen years is a long time to be writing fiction four times a week. In America, it will be a whole new ball game. No one in the States is interested in European politics, but everyone around the world wants to know what is going on with the Kennedys."

"You'll be giving up a lot," she replied. "You own Paris. Washington is full of newspapermen and columnists who could eat you for breakfast."

"I'm willing to gamble, if you are," I said.

"How about this?" Ann said. "Why don't you announce that you're coming back for two years. Then if it doesn't work out, you can return without your tail between your legs."

"That makes sense. I know John Crosby is very unhappy in New York. He keeps taking potshots at Cardinal Spellman and J. Edgar Hoover, and he's driving Jock Whitney's people crazy. I'll ask him if he wants to switch jobs for a couple of years."

When I broached the idea to the *Tribune* powers, they considered my offer a godsend. Crosby, who was *very* unhappy, thought so, too. I owed John a lot. When the *Herald Tribune* had first started syndicating my column, I'd alternated with Crosby on the split page of the paper. People had loved Crosby but had no idea who I was. But they'd assumed since I was in his spot on the alternate days, it was okay to read me. John was always very generous to me right from the start, when it counted the most. He'd also made me change my writing style from third person to first person. It was one of the best things that happened to my career.

I told a few close friends what I was up to. I confided in Irwin Shaw, Teddy White, Larry Collins of *Newsweek*, and Stanley Marcus. Almost to a man, everyone advised me not to do it, though a few, like Dick Wald, the *Trib*'s London bureau chief, thought it was worth a try. They argued that my name was too synonymous with Paris. It wasn't that people wanted to read me in Europe. They *had* to. My secretary, Ursula, also advised me to give it a try. After listening to everybody's view on my move, I pretended that I wasn't scared when, in effect, I was very apprehensive.

Ann confessed to me later that she also was frightened but didn't want to appear so, because it would scare me. The children, who had been to the United States to visit their grandmother several times, and also to become naturalized American citizens, thought moving back was a good idea. There was absolutely nothing on French television that came close to what was being shown back home.

The Paris edition of the *Herald Tribune* was unhappy about my move, because

I had become such a fixture on the paper.

Ann and I agreed to leave at the beginning of September so there would not be an orgy of farewell parties. (Everyone went away for the month of August, so no one could plan anything.)

Once the decision had been made, and I knew in my heart that I would never go back to being a Paris columnist, emotions of an impending loss welled up. Every time I went to Fouquet's or another café, I felt it was for the last time. The Champs-Elysées, which I had taken for granted, was now an old friend on whom I was turning my back. There wasn't a park or building that I didn't make a mental image of in my head.

Each section of the city was a separate chapter in my life. The first one was Montparnasse, where I'd played out my student days. I would call this "A Prince of a Student." On a last farewell tour, I noticed that not much had changed in fourteen years. The cafés were in place — the art students looked no different than the ones I had known when I'd first hung out there.

The Hôtel des États-Unis, which had

been turned into a student dormitory, looked just as dowdy. There was no longer a bar, but in my head I saw ours — I heard the piano music, I saw Kiki dancing on a table, and I felt the same buzz in the air as I listened to young students sitting around telling lies.

All of it was in my imagination. The only thing that was real was the *pissoir.*

The next era of my life was the avenue George-V and the apartment at 24, rue de Boccador. (It meant so much to me I named my pension plan after it.) It was here that life in Paris had become serious. First there was the live-in arrangement with Ann, and the pals who became lifelong friends, and finally the *Herald Tribune*, the paper responsible for all my success in adult life.

This scene was followed by the quai d'Orsay, where Ann and I had set up house and adopted Joel. I would title this one "Life Along the Seine on $20 a Day."

The final chapter would be "Life on the Right Bank Amongst the Swells." Here's where Ann and I had raised our family, thrown parties, and enjoyed a luxurious lifestyle which we could never really afford. I would name this "The

Phantom of the Parc Monceau."

One of the saddest parts of going back to the U.S. was leaving Ursula, who had been my nanny for four years. Ursula, who had two children by the time I left, had no idea what she would do. She wound up working for the Paris office of *Reader's Digest*, and became their best researcher in Europe.

Eric Hawkins had retired and had written a book about the *Herald Tribune.* I missed him very much, because he was such a good friend, and one of the most professional newspapermen I had ever known.

Many of our friends had returned home. One evening a group of former expatriates were sitting around George Plimpton's apartment in New York, and the question was asked what had made each person come home? The consensus was that those who'd come back wanted to be a part of something. France, while a wonderful country, belonged to somebody else. It was no fun fighting French political battles. We acknowledged that each of us had been drawn back by some invisible patriotic magnet, and while we had traded the life of wine and roses for Budweiser and yellow daffodils, we agreed that we had done the right thing.

Each time I have visited Paris since 1962, I have been saddened to find that I had lost another friend. Many returned to the United States — others were dead. The last time I was there, in 1994, I saw Charles Torem, a lawyer who had been one of my first friends in Paris and one of my last. He died last year.

Whenever I saw Charlie, we renewed a wager. If I brought up the name of someone during lunch and that person had died, I had to give Charlie $10. As time went by, my lunches were costing me $230.

I will always go back, but I know that a beautiful city like Paris has to be enjoyed with someone you love. There is so much to do and so much to see that the magic must be shared.

I shared my Paris history almost exclusively with Ann. It is painful to revisit, because I want to turn to her and say, "Remember when we gave the children a party in the Bois de Boulogne, and six-year-old Hat Ascerelli took off all her clothes and stuck her tongue out at the police?

"There's the store where you bought the music box which refused to work when you got it home, and the proprietor said it was your fault."

The French are sentimental. On a recent visit to Paris, I went back to Taillevent, one of the city's most costly but superb restaurants. After a wonderful meal, I called for the check. When it arrived, written across the top was "Compliments of the House." This startled me, and I called the owner to ask for an explanation. He said, "When you lived in Paris, you were always nice to my father and I have waited a long time to repay you."

The ghosts are everywhere — the memories remain vivid, sometimes painful and sometimes exploding, making me want to cry.

The last two months for me were the toughest. Paris is not an easy city to leave.

One of the recurring topics of conversation at that time was whether I would fall flat on my face in the U.S. Most people seemed to be predicting that I would. I was a big wheel in the newspaper world in Europe. Now I was going back and would have to fight it out with the pros — Lippman, Alsop, Drew Pearson. The pessimists around me pointed out that I knew nothing about American politics and I had no idea what made the American reader laugh. Ben Bradlee claims that he urged me to come back to the U.S. I'll give him the credit for this, in exchange for him giving me Frank Frigenti.

Amid all the turmoil of emotions about returning to the States, something else was going on of which I was unaware. I was beginning to slide into a depression. Subconsciously, the cure for it was for me to go home in the hopes that it would simply go away. Things were piling up on me, and I seemed to be discontented with many aspects of my life. My trips ceased to be exciting, and the column sounded tired. I went to see Jean Dax, and he prescribed some medication to help calm me down. But I was hell-bent on heading for my mid-life crisis.

Soon after I returned in 1963, I did in fact have a serious clinical depression. Everything seemed to come crashing down. With hospitalization and some wonderful medical help, I recovered, and only then did I understand why something other than my work was calling me home.

During our final days in Paris, Ann and I were already reminiscing about this city that we had fallen in love with — over and over again. She would say, "I will miss the smells. I was in the market today and I was astonished by how many aromas there were, from the cheeses to fish to meat to fresh bread. It was intoxicating."

I told her, "It sounds weird, but I'll miss the noises. The automobile honking that drives me nuts — the church bells ringing at all hours, and the police klaxons. It took me fourteen years to get used to the hubbub of Paris, and now we won't hear it any more."

She said, "I know you're going to think I'm crazy, but one of the things I'm going to miss the most is the asparagus."

"Hot or cold?"

She said, "The cold ones. I love them with vinaigrette."

I said, "I prefer the hot ones, served with a béarnaise sauce. I always had to get my tie cleaned after I ate them."

"Do you ever think we'll taste French melon again?"

"I'd settle for the strawberries with crème fraîche."

"Don't even mention chicken in a paper bag from the Tour d'Argent."

"I won't, if you promise not to talk about the fresh pasta with seafood at Chez Righi."

I asked Ann, "Did we ever make love under the Pont-Neuf?"

She said, "You wanted to, but I refused to, because it was raining."

I sighed. "I'm sorry we're leaving without ever having done that. It's my favorite bridge."

"You also wanted to make love in the Tuileries on our second date."

"That would have been nice. What happened?"

"We were wrestling on a bench, when a policeman came by and waved his baton back and forth, as if to say, 'Just so far, mes enfants.' "

"We're lucky he was French. The cops in Central Park would have used their blackjacks on me . . ."

Ann said, "The place you got the friskiest was the Rodin Museum."

"I guess I was inspired by *The Kiss.*"

In seventy years on this earth, everyone is going to have ups and downs. I have had my share, but what I find interesting is that most of my ups have been connected to my downs, which have resulted in the sad episodes of my life having happy endings.

One of the downers of my life was being a ward of the Hebrew Orphan Asylum in New York and then living in a series of foster homes. The upper aspect of this experience was when I was invited to speak at the 150th anniversary of the Jewish Child Care Association in New York.

I jumped at the idea of standing up in the ballroom of the Pierre Hotel and addressing all the people who at one time or another had been in charge of my life. Many of those in the audience were from the "Our Crowd" New York Jewish community, and I had always been in awe of them. But on this occasion, instead of treating me as a waif, they looked on me as one of their successful sons. After I finished my speech, I received a standing ovation.

Another time when I rose successfully from a downer was when I was invited to address the U.S. Marine Aviation Association at their annual banquet. I had been a lousy ordnance man in the Marine Corps. I was a questionable rifleman and was known as someone who could not be trusted to load a bomb. But at the banquet, I was presented with a plaque stating that I had been a great Marine.

It was a wonderful feeling for me to address that roomful of officers and their wives. I reveled in the respect they showed me — respect that I had never gotten as a Sergeant in the VMF-113 fighter squadron.

I didn't graduate from high school or college. So my next big thrill came when the University of Southern California presented me with an Honorary Doctorate of Letters and also asked me to be their graduation speaker. I addressed an assembled crowd of 32,000 graduates and their proud families.

I told the students that based on my own educational record, all of them had wasted their time. I got another standing ovation.

But I think that my greatest moment of glory came in 1987. The *Herald Tribune* was celebrating its one hundredth anniversary, and publisher Lee Huebner and editor John Vinocur invited me to come back as the grand guest of honor. I immediately accepted. I loved the idea that I was looked upon as the Rip Van Winkle of the paper.

The celebration was to take place in Paris in October, and I was to speak at various functions throughout the week, including the major banquet to be held in a specially constructed tent at the Palais de Chaillot with its spectacular view of the Eiffel Tower across the Seine. There were 1,600 guests.

This is why it was such an upper. Two years before this event, I received a call from the Los Angeles Times Syndicate which distributes my column. The caller said, "Do you know that when you left the Paris *Trib* in 1962, they agreed to pay thirty-five dollars for the column. It is now 1985, and they are still paying thirty-five. I think we should ask them for seventy."

I told him it sounded reasonable to me.

The next day, he called again and said, "They're balking at a raise. Do you want to go to the mattress on this?"

"Hell, no. I'll pay them seventy to keep the column in the paper."

They finally settled on $50 a week —

the price of a glass of table wine at Maxim's.

But I was about to have my revenge. The invitation to Paris included two seats for Ann and myself on the Concorde, a suite at the Ritz Hotel, and a chauffeur-driven car at our disposal for the length of our stay. As I sat on the Concorde, I recalled another trip to Paris years ago. It was a Pan Am flight and Charles Lindbergh was sitting across from me. He was a member of the airline's board. I fought a battle with myself — do I ask him how he liked flying a jet or should I respect his privacy? I finally opted to stay quiet, and it was a decision I have always regretted. I'm sure that the world would have given anything to know what was going through Lindbergh's mind as we flew east at five hundred miles an hour and ate food prepared by Maxim's.

The big night came. I was the major speaker. I was also flesh and blood — the connection between the old paper and present one. I can't think of any newspaperman who could have had a greater opportunity to fulfill a dream of glory.

The *Trib* staff had been invited, as had

the diplomatic and business communities in Europe. There were bigshots from the French government, as well as the major advertisers. Newspaper alumni were also there, like Bernie Cutler, Don Cook, Willet Weeks, Sylvan Barnett, and Brown Reid. The guests also included friends like Helmut Schmidt, Donald Graham, Ben Bradlee, and Sally Quinn.

Ann was seated on my right and, at my request, Ursula on my left. The French minister of defense was seated across from us. Ursula, never impressed by rank, spoke to him. "Monsieur, my son is a draftee in the Army and your men keep beating him up."

The minister blushed and finally said, "Are you sure, madame, you wish to discuss this matter at the table?"

Ursula responded, "Why not? This may be the only chance I get to talk to you."

I kicked Ursula under the table, but she seemed very pleased with herself. When she got home and told her son what she had done, he turned white and yelled, "Momma, now I am really going to get it."

I gave my speech, and because the

occasion was so meaningful to me, I delivered it with great feeling.

The highlight of the evening was the moment a gigantic cake with ninety-nine candles was wheeled out onto the dance floor. Dick Morgan, the MC, said, "I want everyone in the room to blow out the candles." We all blew, and the candles went out. "Now for the hundredth candle." We blew again, and all the Eiffel Tower lights went out! It was the *Tribune*'s hundredth candle.

I don't think that anything could compare to that week in Paris. The combination of the time, the place, the people — in my heart I knew that there would never be another celebration like this, because there would never be another occasion like this one.

So, it came time to leave. Ann and I were all packed. I have no idea what was going on in other people's minds at the *Trib* that morning, but I had great questions whirling around in mine about whether I was doing the right thing.

At the Gare St-Lazare, we sat on our luggage, waiting for the boat train to take us to the *Queen Mary* at Le Havre and home. There were six of us. Ann and myself, the three children, and our Irish nurse, Kay. We had fifteen pieces of luggage.

When Ann and I had arrived separately fourteen years earlier, we had each had one bag and hardly any money. Paris had been extremely kind to us and would leave its mark on us forever. Tears were shed by Ann and myself and the friends who came to say good-bye.

When we were making arrangements for her funeral in 1994, our son Joel suggested that since Paris had played such a significant role in Ann's life, we ask the church soloist to sing the *Marseillaise* at the end of the service. She did. It was the perfect tribute to Ann, and to Paris, which had given both of us so many glorious years.

The employees of Thorndike Press hope you have enjoyed this Large Print book. All our Large Print titles are designed for easy reading, and all our books are made to last. Other Thorndike Large Print books are available at your library, through selected bookstores, or directly from us.

For information about titles, please call:

(800) 223-2336

To share your comments, please write:

Publisher
Thorndike Press
P.O. Box 159
Thorndike, Maine 04986